Change Change

Introducing the Art of Transformagination®

Neil Butler

The Rural Publishing Company

Cover Design: The Rural Publishing Company
Typesetting & Design: The Rural Publishing Company

The Rural Publishing Company
Website: https://theruralpublishingcompany.com.au
Email: hello@theruralpublishingcompany.com.au

Contents

Acknowledgements

Books like these don't just write themselves.

Firstly, I would like to thank all of my colleagues and associates with whom I have discussed the concept of Transformagination® – you know who you are. This is a concept that needed to be bounced around with people who know me and who know change. Thanks for your guidance and advice.

A special thanks to Scott – the colleague who bought me a beer at The Garden State Hotel in Melbourne in 2019 and who was the first one to enthusiastically agree that Transformagination® should be a thing. Here we are, all those years later, with a book and a website!

To my colleagues and leaders in the various places I have worked, from the very good to the downright ordinary. Each of you has, in some small way, contributed to my development and taught me something about change, about transformation and indeed, about the corporate world in which we have worked together.

And, before I go, I'd better say hello to Maverick and Ned – two young lads who will hopefully be excited to see their names in Pop's book.

Introduction

So, why write a book?

I suspect that it's a bit like being a songwriter. An idea pops into your head and, until you actually sit down and metaphorically put pen to paper, it will swirl around and around in there until you actually **do** sit down and metaphorically put pen to paper.

There are many, many business books out there with a substantial number of them dealing with change management. This, of course, begs the question of why I would try to impact on an already saturated market.

Well, apart from that whole swirling thing I mentioned a couple of paragraphs ago, I am hoping to bring ideas that are not dependent upon following a particular methodology but rather to try and change a mindset – indeed, to **change** change.

The other thing that I hope you'll notice as you work your way through this book is that, beyond some very thorough proofreading to check my spelling and grammar, it has not been edited by a publisher or any other person apart from me. I can most assuredly confirm that no artificial intelligence machine has been harmed in the writing of this book (except for some brief observations in Chapter 7 – more about that later).

No, simply **my** thoughts, written in **my** words and not tainted by any other influence, outside of the occasional credited quote from someone more intelligent or talented than me.

And yes, there is a healthy dose of common sense and 'stating the bleeding obvious' in what follows but sadly, from my experience, far too many books on this and similar topics, focus heavily on introducing new concepts and methodologies, while overlooking what's right there in front of us. Yes, we'll introduce a new concept (see next paragraph) but we'll deal with some basics up front.

The book is broadly divided into three main sections – the first section discussing **change**, the second presenting **transformation** and finally, I will introduce the concept of **Transformagination**® in the third part of the book.

As well, I have added a section towards the end of the book

that covers some broader ideas and principles that I have gathered or developed along the way. While not necessarily belonging in a book about changing change, I figured that while you were here and in a mindset for challenge, I would share those as well.

There is probably some advantage in reading the book from start to finish in the sequence presented, if only to get a sense of how I have developed my thinking. That said, the book has been designed for you to pick up and read as and when you get the chance and almost as a series of related articles.

This book is intended to challenge and to make existing change practitioners feel a little uncomfortable. Clearly, not everything in this book will work in every circumstance nor for everyone engaged in delivering change.

If, however, having read this book, you decide to adjust your approach to delivering change or transformation or you start to move your mindset towards **Transformagination**®, it will have been worth the time we have both invested.

So, with all that in mind, please join me as we set about trying to **change change**.

Chapter 1

Change

Let's start by providing my definition of change – it may not be the dictionary definition, but here's mine:

Change is the act of making something different to what it was before.

Nothing more than that. Change can be intentional and it can be accidental. Change can happen deliberately because it is needed but, equally, it can happen unexpectedly due to factors you have no control over.

The example I like to use to describe change in a corporate environment is painting the wall of a meeting room green when, up until this point in time, it has been the usual, dull and uninspiring beige, favoured in so many offices around the world.

To effect this change, we will need the meeting room to be unavailable for a day or two (hopefully the painters will work over the weekend to reduce the impact on the business). Maybe the only action required by the change team is to send an email to all impacted colleagues, letting them know to make other arrangements if they had been planning to use the room.

Sure, some changes are bigger than the one in my example, but the idea is still the same – **we are making something different to what it was before**. We need to let people know what's happening and how it will impact on them. We need to plan ahead to ensure that the change impact is minimised.

But, at the end of the day, **we are simply making something different to what it was**.

Myth: People dislike and/or fear change

I really don't think people are uncomfortable with change. It is a common perception that people dislike change. You might even find that people tell you that they don't like change, but I think they are wrong.

No, I think people dislike and/or fear **uncertainty**.

I think of it as **TRAUMATIC** – The Real Anxiety Uncertainty Might Actually Trigger In Colleagues.

When you think about it, we encounter change hundreds of times a day. We change our location. We change our clothes. We change the contents of our fridge whenever we eat or drink something. We change our bank balance when we buy something.

In each case, we are implementing or experiencing change but change that we have certainty about.

Think about change in the context of travelling. In fact, I am writing this section of the book on an aeroplane flying from Melbourne to Delhi to complete some work for a client. This is my second visit to the same office, working with the same people. Last time I visited, there was apprehension because I had no idea what to expect at the other end. My client had provided enough information to mitigate most of my anxiety but there was still that lingering feeling as we touched down.

Of course, I need not have worried, but the fact that my surroundings were about to change from the very familiar to the completely unknown provided me with some degree of discomfort.

On this occasion, however – my second visit to the same city and to spend time with the same people – that feeling of anxiety has not surfaced because there is significantly less **uncertainty**.

Don't buy into the myth that people dislike or fear change. Remove the **uncertainty** and watch the fear and anxiety levels reduce.

Removing the uncertainty

Maybe easier said than done, but this is where the strategic thinking needs to kick in.

Take some time to understand the factors that are creating the uncertainty – timing, the reasons for the change, likely outcomes, impact on the individual, organisational structure, maybe something else?

As you'll read in the next section, there is no single 'silver bullet' for removing uncertainty but one thing you can be sure of is this:

> *Uncertainty is maximised wherever and whenever transparency is minimised.*

And before you say it, yes, I get it – some change programs require confidentiality during the planning and, often, during the early stages of implementing the change.

But here's the thing – **confidentiality and transparency are not mutually exclusive**. They can co-exist in any change program, as far as I can see.

Take a corporate organisational restructure, for example. Peak uncertainty leading to peak anxiety – or is it? Yes, there needs to be confidentiality around roles and individuals during the planning stages but that doesn't preclude transparency around timing, for example.

If people are checking their emails three times a day to see whether there is an update about the restructure, when there isn't an update, their thoughts may well turn to 'why aren't they telling us anything' or 'when will we know' or a million other things.

Instead, letting people know that the next update will be at a particular time or date reduces that anxiety around uncertainty. Of course, the challenge in that approach is that, if you do make a commitment to update people at a certain time or date, you better make sure you do!

Take a look at the section below called **Managing Expectations**.

One size fits one

I have always been fascinated by the concept of one size fits all. One such example is the ubiquitous baseball cap that most people have in their collection of headwear.

Many of these caps have 'One Size Fits All' emblazoned on the manufacturer's label.

When I went to buy my first Akubra hat, I fronted up to the rural clothing store and placed a size 60 hat on my head. When both the shopkeeper and I agreed that this was not even close to being big enough for my head, he had to place a special order for a size 63 to be manufactured especially for me.

It appears that those 'One Size Fits All' caps are made to stretch out, maybe to a size 60, with elastic providing the flexibility to reduce its size down to any smaller adult head. Try stretching it beyond that size to fit someone like me!

So, maybe, they should be marked with 'One Size Fits Most' or 'One Size Fits Some' because they certainly don't fit me!

Unfortunately, I have seen and been involved in far too many projects where change planning falls into the 'One Size Fits All' category. One-way, same-way Change Management.

Unsurprisingly, this approach rarely works, certainly not on larger or more complex change projects.

Each individual who is impacted by a change will be impacted in a different way and to varying degrees. Different levels of anxiety, based on the various factors that are important to them and how much those factors will change.

While it may not be practical to individualise a change plan for each impacted person, especially for larger programs of work that impact larger cohorts of people, each individual's needs must at least be considered.

Don't go into your program expecting your high-level, 'one way, same way' change plan to work for every single person. Work on the basis that one size fits one and if it fits **some**, that is a massive bonus.

Managing Expectations

You take your car in for a new set of tyres. You choose the brand and model of tyres you want to have fitted and head home, expecting that you'll get a call to pick the car up later that afternoon.

2 o'clock. No call.

4:30pm. Still no call.

You are becoming mildly agitated by this stage because you are heading out for dinner and you need your car. You call the tyre place at 5:00pm and they tell you the car won't be ready until at least lunchtime in a couple of days.

But why are you getting upset? The tyre business knew that they had to order the tyres and that it was going to take three or four days before you got your car back. They didn't bother to tell you because they knew and probably assumed you did too. They may even believe that they told you there would be a delay.

The reason you are getting upset is this – **you set your own expectation** and when the tyre business failed to meet **your** expectations, you got mad.

There is a significant lesson here for your next change activity.

Get on the front foot and not only set the expectations, announce those expectations early and clearly. Tell people what they should expect. Tell them when their next update will happen. Tell them what the post-change world looks like. Don't assume that they have heard the message, even though you are pretty certain that you told the impacted individuals what to expect.

And, of course, invite consultation around those

expectations. Don't assume that (a) everyone is on the same page as you nor (b) assume that your page is the correct page for everyone. Consultation should be a two-way street and, if done properly, you'll know whether everyone's expectations are aligned.

Going back to the car analogy, if you had known when you dropped the car off that it would be a few days before you were going to be able to pick it up, you certainly wouldn't be concerned when you hadn't received a call back by the end of the first day. You would have made alternative plans for your dinner appointment and for getting to where you had to be during the following couple of days.

Who's at fault in this situation? Maybe the tyre people for not telling you when to expect the car back. Maybe it is your fault for not asking.

Either way, the lesson is clear – **set** expectations, **agree** expectations and **announce** expectations. Open the door for discussions and consultation to ensure that everyone knows where, what, when, how and why a change will occur **before** you get started.

And one last thing about consultation. Many programs of work involve a designated consultation period, especially ones that create organisational change. Do you **consult** or do you **announce** and wait for feedback?

Most dictionary definitions of **consultation** include a reference to a discussion. Consultation needs to be proactive and not just a tick-box activity. It needs more than an announcement followed by an opportunity to send an email to the program team.

Actively engage with those who are impacted and listen to their concerns and suggestions. They might have some valuable input that will improve the program's outcomes and/or minimise the anxiety for impacted colleagues.

Change Management

This is a term that I really don't like. **Change Management**.

I am okay with the **change** bit – it is the management bit I am less enthusiastic about. Management has overtones of control and so it feels to me a bit like we are stifling the flow a little here.

I absolutely agree that having a change approach that everyone agrees on – and is prepared to follow – is a really important component of a successful project.

But I much prefer **Change Leadership** (and I am not just talking semantics here). I recall a poster on the wall of my people leader's office many years ago that said:

'A leader is someone who knows the way, shows the way and then goes the way.'

Isn't this what we want from our change colleagues? Someone who knows where the organisation is going, shows the impacted people where we are all going and, finally, leads the way for everyone.

Another philosophy that I was exposed to at around the same time is that:

'Managers manage things while leaders lead people.'

Many Change Managers seem to think that the most important factor in delivering a successful change program is a solid, heavily documented, change plan. Don't get me wrong – developing a plan to deliver the change has enormous benefits and is something that every project requires.

But … **and it's a really important but** … the people involved in the change are **so much more important** than the plan itself. It may seem odd that I have to point this out but believe me, this call out is necessary for many change practitioners I have worked with.

I have worked with Change Managers who seriously believe that the most important thing they can do is to create a massive PowerPoint pack, full of theories and diagrams that add no value (and often make no sense), that will impress the responsible executives and the rest of the project leadership team.

Be honest with yourself. When you last created one of those packs, how often and how much of the pack did you review and revise after the initial version? Did you ever feel the need to sit down and work your way through the methodology slides with a colleague? Did the Kübler-Ross curve that you so dutifully included in the pack ever get referenced by you or any of your colleagues during the lifecycle of the project?

Change plans often get developed and stored away, never to see the light of day again. The Change Manager ticks the Change Plan off the to-do list and never refers to it afterwards.

It seems that the Change Plan is able to look after itself from that point. The people who are being impacted by the change … not so much.

If we agree that it is the people who are the more important factor in a change program (and, most certainly, they must be), why are we not putting more emphasis on Change Leadership instead of Change Management?

As an aside and to make the terminology clear, in many organisations, the term Change Lead is used but only in the context of the person responsible for a bunch of other Change Managers. That's not the same thing – **Change Lead does not equal Change Leader.**

We need significantly less management of change. Instead, let us hear of – and strongly encourage – more leadership of change, please.

Change or Challenge?

If you look at these two words, they are very similar in their spelling – indeed, add three letters to **change** and you get **challenge**.

So, what can the additional three letters – **lle** – bring to the conversation?

The first L can be leadership. As you will find throughout this book, the concept of change leadership – not change management – throughout a change program is a key to success.

The second L can be limitless. As you work your way through this book, you'll see that I am really big on removing limits. Limits get in the way. Limits stop us from achieving greatness.

And then there is the additional E. **E is for excellence.** We want excellence to be our goal in everything we do as change leaders. If we strive for anything less than excellence, we are far more likely to achieve that reduced expectation but **significantly** less likely to deliver our outcomes successfully.

So, don't be fixated on change. Think challenge. Be the person in the room who wants to ask the hard questions. Be the one who **leads** the way. Be the one who tries to work around the **limits** to achieve greatness. Be the one who strives for **excellence** in everything we set out to achieve.

Be **a challenge leader** not just **a change manager**.

Get On the Front Foot

The other thing about leadership when compared to management is the need to be on the front foot. When I think about **leading** something, it speaks to me of someone knowing where they are going and heading off towards that destination (more about that in the next section).

Often, change occurs for unforeseen reasons and in response to an activity or event that comes as something of a surprise. In this circumstance, you find yourself on the back foot and, in cricketing parlance, defending a short ball from within your crease.

In many instances, you will find yourself on the back foot through no fault of your own. That said, doing whatever you can to get yourself on the front foot is a worthwhile investment of time and energy.

Leadership in change is so much more effective than management of change. Leadership allows self-determination of outcomes. Leadership allows you to set the agenda.

Management sounds much more like trying to keep things under control. Management seems to involve setting up guardrails to stop the program of work going off course.

Don't get me wrong – there are times when back foot management is needed in the short term, especially where things have changed due to unexpected events.

Your aim, though, should be to get off the back foot, onto the front foot and start leading change. It might mean taking a day or two, maybe a week, to take a breath and to set your own agenda. Being proactive instead of reactive.

Trust me – it will be worth the effort.

Destination: Somewhere

Are we there yet?

If you have ever been on a long road trip, especially with younger family members who don't appreciate your selection of music, you will dread hearing those four words … **are we there yet?**

Too often, change programs kick off with only a vague idea of where the program is headed. Deploy this software. Release a new product into the market. Open a new shop somewhere in the city.

If your outcomes are vague, your approach to delivering that change will be equally vague.

Let's consider an analogy of a family driving from Melbourne to Sydney for a holiday. If we get in the car early one morning, the inevitable cries of 'are we there yet' will kick in sooner or later. If we know we are staying in accommodation over the road from Manly's iconic wharf, we can plan out the trip ahead and, with the assistance of a GPS/maps app, we can accurately predict arrival time, the route we need to take, etc.

If, however, the best we have is 'staying somewhere in Sydney', we'll get to the outskirts of the city and have no real idea of where the journey will end. If we get to Campbelltown, are we in Sydney? Do we need to get to the Opera House to know we have arrived?

A vague destination leads to confusion and an inability to know when the journey will end. A clear statement of destination (in the business sense, this translates to a set of clear statements of what successful completion looks like) will provide certainty for everyone involved.

It just might even stop people asking if we are there yet.

Another Myth: Change Is Difficult

Change isn't difficult at all. That said, for many people, **acceptance** of change **can be** difficult.

As I suggested earlier, we are surrounded by change, and we have been since the day we were born. As the great John Denver sang 'I guess growing isn't hard to do, just stand against a wall. Once I was just two feet high, today I'm six feet tall.'

We see the day become night and the night become day. Every day.

We change jobs, we move house. We buy new cars and spend time in different holiday destinations.

These are all changes that we deal with every day. Some are thrust upon us, and some are our own choice.

So why are some changes easier to accept and deal with than others?

The following is by no means an exhaustive list, but I think getting these things right will help people accept change more readily than they otherwise would.

Let's start with something we spoke of earlier – **removing uncertainty**. People are far more likely to move towards a different situation if they are **certain** about an outcome. If you were 100% certain that a new job was going to work out for you, would you be more or less likely to leave your current role to take it on?

If you were asked to invest in a business, would you be more or less likely to invest if you were 100% certain that the business was going to be successful?

Many organisations like to talk about reducing risk. While in this case, I am playing semantics, I would prefer to talk about the positive step of **creating certainty** rather than **reducing risk**. It has a much more positive tone for me.

Next up is engagement. You'll notice a deliberate choice to use **engagement** instead of **communication** in this context (more about this in a later section). Engagement is about building relationships whereas communication is about telling people something (and hoping they are listening).

Engaging with impacted people when leading a change program means building a relationship with them and giving them an opportunity to participate in conversations. This is one of the primary reasons social media has been successful. Websites often provide information via text, videos, brochures, pictures, etc. but, except for the 'Contact Us' page, there is often no real opportunity to **engage**.

Social media, on the other hand, provides a platform for a business, an organisation, a club or an individual to engage with their followers. It allows comments to be left and responded to. It allows us to build relationships through two-way conversations.

Have you noticed that two of the most traditional forms of non-printed communication – radio and television – have ditched their old-fashioned 'one-way' formats and have replaced them with opportunities for viewers/listeners to

engage? Whether that is via talkback, live crosses, messages via SMS or other messaging channels, the best radio and television now occurs when people can actively participate either during a program or via the socials after the event.

In the context of many change projects, the 'comms team' produce a plethora of written materials, sent around via email, expecting people to read the content. This is the equivalent of printing a whole lot of brochures and throwing them over a fence, hoping that someone picks one up and reads it.

Think about your inbox.

What proportion of the emails you receive are straight text on a white background in black 11pt Aptos font (or whatever font your laptop is defaulting to)? How many have the word 'Update' in the subject line? How many of these do you bother to read and digest?

And yet, you keep sending emails out as your primary mechanism for keeping people informed. If you are not **engaging** with the recipients, you have no guarantee that the messaging has been received, much less read and absorbed.

I have been in the corporate world since before email was a thing. Trust me when I say that **no one** has ever said they want to receive **more** emails (maybe, back in 1991 when there was still a novelty factor in receiving an 'electronic mail message' – but not since then).

More of the same is not a way to attract the attention of your recipients.

Be creative. Use different channels to **engage**. Don't waste your time trying to lead people through a change by sending one-way messages without an opportunity for the recipients to continue a conversation.

It saddens me to have to even suggest this but **telling the truth** is also really important. I know that we have all been told to tell the truth ever since we were first admonished for making a mess, when one of our siblings sustained a mystery injury or when we were asked if we had done our homework.

And yet, here we are as grown-ups having to be reminded to tell the truth when we are engaging with people who are going to be impacted by a change project.

While it is important to maintain confidentiality during certain phases of some projects, this does not give us the green light to be untruthful.

I have been impacted by several projects over the years where the communication (yes, not engagement) has been a collection of complete and deliberate untruths. Misleading impacted people is not only wrong in its primary sense, but it also leads to an erosion of trust and credibility.

Next, **be with the people who are impacted**. How often do you see a project team sitting in a closed project room and never venturing out to sit with the people who are going to have to accept the change that they are about to deliver?

To lead people through the acceptance of a change, regardless of how minor the change might seem to you, you need to be part of the scene, not tucked away in a project room, away from the main game. Understand how they are feeling by talking with them. Never be accused of sitting in an ivory tower (as an aside, has anyone actually ever been to a real ivory tower?).

Finally, **remember who the important people are**. It may come as a surprise to some that the project team for a change project are NOT the important people. Neither are the sponsors of the project or the executive who set the project up.

No, the important people are those whose role is about to change. Who may be about to lose their job. Who may have to learn a new system or process. Who may need to build new relationships.

The important people are **not** the senior managers who will tick off on the business case. The important people are **not** the consultants and contractors who come in, design and/or deliver the change and walk away. The important people are most certainly **NOT** the project team.

As someone once said, it's nice to be important but it's more important to be nice. Don't overplay your importance – instead, be nice to those who are.

Here are five things to remember:

1. Create certainty.

2. Engage.

3. Be truthful.

4. Get among it.

5. Remember who is important.

Do these five things and you will certainly make change easier to accept.

What Happens If It Goes ~~Wrong~~ Right?

We have addressed the question of risk management elsewhere in the book, but it is worth spending a few moments on this here.

Risk management is usually predicated on the 'what happens if it goes wrong' or 'what's the worst thing that could happen' approach.

Acknowledging the importance of managing risks, if done sensibly and creatively, risks can be mitigated, allowing the program of work to proceed, albeit with suitable checks and balances in place to minimise the likelihood of things going wrong.

My concern here, though, is that these two questions are often used as an excuse to keep doing what we have always done. If we spend enough time focusing on what could go wrong or what the worst outcome could be, it is going to set up an ideal platform for continuing to do what we have always done.

Opening our minds to what could happen if it goes **right** and the **best** thing that could happen – that is, the direct opposite – provides a platform for creating change, for moving forward, for taking the naysayers on a journey towards doing things differently.

This doesn't mean that we go out, all guns blazing, and **hoping** for the best. That would be irresponsible. What it does mean is that, if we want to move our organisation forward, to doing things differently, there needs to be a balance between looking at what could go **right**, not just **wrong**. A balance between the **best** thing that could happen, not just the **worst**.

Change Management and Methodologies

I am old enough to remember when Change Management wasn't even a thing. Back then, we tried to make sure that changes were implemented successfully and then, we got on and trained people if there were new things to learn. I guess we were leading change – it just wasn't called that in those days.

But along came Change Management, with its upper case 'C' and upper case 'M'. It became a thing, maybe in the early 1990s. Sure, we had been managing change for centuries, but it was around this time when the consulting firms got hold of it.

People started using the job title 'Change Manager' and with that came a whole range of methodologies and accreditations. Some protocols have stayed the distance, and some have fallen by the wayside.

Don't get me wrong – I have also used the title 'Change Manager' on my resume and have watched as we have moved from delivering change to Change Management.

Many of my colleagues and associates have used these prescribed methodologies to create a structured approach to successfully deliver change. So, they absolutely work.

However, in other circumstances, I have seen Change Managers – and the organisations they work in – paralysed by the need to follow **every single step** in their preferred methodology, regardless of the scope, size and style of the change project. It is as though they think that delivering a beautifully constructed change plan – with all of its associated artefacts – is more important than successfully delivering the outcomes of the project.

As you can probably tell, I don't subscribe to this approach. Yes, we absolutely need a planned, documented approach to delivering change. What we don't need is a SharePoint folder full of documents that no one reads.

I have worked with people and in organisations that believe that this is the right way to approach change. Leaders demand a 'BIA' which, for many practitioners, is a spreadsheet with a whole lot of ticks (or maybe, traffic lights!) against different individuals or teams. Leaders ask for a 'RACI' which, more often than not, gets written, inserted in the change plan and never sees the light of day again. They insist on creating a 'comms plan' which, as we will discuss later, is pointless unless it is part of a broader engagement activity.

So much effort goes into creating these artefacts that, in many cases, their usefulness becomes limited. The completion of each of these artefacts often defines the milestones and stage gates for the project, rather than the delivery of the change itself.

Instead of delivering an artefact called a BIA (in case you are wondering, that's a Business Impact Assessment or Analysis, depending on which protocols you are following), let's focus our attention on the actual assessment. Who is this change impacting on? How is this change impacting on them? What do we need to do to mitigate risks? What steps can we take to remove uncertainty?

Instead of delivering a RACI (Responsible, Accountable, Consult, Inform) matrix – usually a spreadsheet – let's understand who needs to do what, who they need to work with and how they will work together.

Now, you might be thinking that all I am doing here is describing the acronyms in more detail and I guess I am to an extent. In fact, though, what I am doing is describing **actions** rather than the **artefacts** that, in many organisations, appear to be the desired outcome.

Artefacts are useless without the actions that they **should**, but often **don't**, generate.

The BIA vs the Business Impact Action Plan

So, let's consider the BIA – the Business Impact Assessment (or Analysis, depending upon which course you completed). As I said in the previous section, the acronym is often used to describe an artefact rather than an activity. A beautifully curated spreadsheet with names or roles down the left-hand side and a whole lot of ticks in boxes. The really fancy ones have these ticks in various coloured boxes – red for serious impact through to green for minor impact.

But that is NOT a Business Impact Assessment. A Business Impact Assessment is a thing you do; it is not an artefact. Yes, the artefact may provide a great summary of some of the learnings gained in completing the assessment, but the assessment is an activity, not an artefact.

From now on, my challenge to you is to complete your BIA (that is, the actual assessment) and develop a new document called a **Business Impact Action Plan**. By all means, analyse the impacts that your change program is going to deliver on your colleagues or clients. You can even record them in a spreadsheet if you want.

But don't make that the end of that road. Don't go and tick the Business Impact Assessment off your to-do list just yet.

Create a Business Impact Action Plan – a document that outlines who is impacted, how they are impacted and … here's the kicker … what you are going to do about it. What actions do you as the change leader need to take to minimise the impact on your colleagues and stakeholders?

Engage – don't enrage

People get grumpy when they feel that change is made without their involvement.

What do you mean, without their involvement – we sent them an email about what we are doing, didn't we?

There is a section later in the book that talks about engagement vs communication and, if you don't know the difference, I'd encourage you to find that section and spend some time reflecting.

There is also the concept of Stakeholder Engagement that gets talked about quite a lot in the context of Change Management – but what do we actually mean?

We don't just mean keeping the key players informed. We don't just mean telling them what we are up to. We mean taking the key people along on the journey with us. No surprises. Transparency – that is what we mean.

If you don't engage properly, people WILL become defensive and probably grumpy, regardless of how big or small the change is that you are proposing.

My tip – engage DON'T enrage!

~~WHFM~~ WIIFT

I might be splitting hairs here, but it is a really important distinction.

As leaders of change, we will often hear that we need to identify the **WIIFM** – the 'What's In It For Me' (who doesn't love a funky acronym?). If we can identify a motivation for our colleagues, clients or other stakeholders to accept our change, it will make our job of delivering change so much easier.

Yes, but we don't necessarily want to make our job easier – we want those people to adopt, accept and embrace the change we are delivering.

So, is it time to focus on WIIFT – What's In It For **Them**?

If we simply impose a change on an individual, a team or an organisation, are we giving them the information they need to absorb and process what is changing?

Take some time to work through what the change means for **them**. It will help in the removal of uncertainty and support your efforts in delivering a change.

So What?

This question represents one half of two of the most important questions a leader of change can ask.

The announcement of an upcoming change – a restructure, a new system, new leadership, a new product range – is usually a major event with emails flying around and town hall meetings being conducted. Within a couple of hours everyone knows what is planned but uncertainty levels are high.

This is when it is really important to ask the question – **so what**? What does this announcement actually mean? For our colleagues? For our customers? For our suppliers? For our organisation's reputation?

Only when we have an answer to **so what** will we be able to develop a strategy and an approach for the delivery of the upcoming change program.

It is such an important question. The sooner we get it answered, the sooner we can start the process of reducing uncertainty and anxiety and the sooner we can get on with change delivery.

Now What?

And here's the other half of the two most important questions a leader of change can ask. We can easily get so bogged down in the **so what** that we forget that, without some kind of action plan, everything grinds to a halt.

Once we know the **why**, the very next thing we need to focus on is the **now what**?

Change plans and strategies are completely pointless if they result in no action. We have already spoken about the Business Impact Action Plan. When you create a Change Plan does it specifically set out actions and who is doing them (and no, a RACI doesn't count – it just tells us who gets the blame if the change doesn't work)?

And how are we going to know if we are successful if we don't have some way to measure those actions? By stating what has to happen, who is going to actually complete those actions and how we can measure success, we can confidently move forward with a very clear picture of **now what**.

My methodology – the A to H Approach

Many years ago, I was chatting to a colleague who told me that not only should I be using a particular change methodology but I should be qualified and accredited by completing a rather expensive training course. At this point, I had been working in the change arena for around 10 years and didn't really feel inclined to spend the hundreds, if not thousands, of dollars it would cost me to get a qualification.

While these courses have their place – especially for people starting out on a career in change management – I have seen several examples of 'qualified change practitioners' managing a change (deliberate use of 'manage') where it seems that completing the processes and artefacts in their 'correct' sequence is more important than the change we are trying to deliver.

When protocols and methodologies are so prescriptive that the change manager cannot deliver their own tailored approach to change and transformation, do projects run more smoothly or delivery occur more successfully? Not in my experience.

That same colleague challenged me to transform what she described as my 'loose approach to change delivery' into something that she could read and follow.

Here's what I came up with – the **A to H Approach**.

A is for Assess

One of my bugbears in the world of change is leaders who tell me what the solution is before we even start – go and implement this system, create this organisational structure, etc.

Going into solution mode at this early stage of play – that is, before we even know what we are trying to achieve – seems counter-intuitive to me.

The first step for me must be to answer this question – **what is the problem we are trying to solve?**

There is a very clear distinction in my mind between **here is a problem we are trying to solve** and **here is a solution I want you to deliver**.

The pre-determined solution is often proposed because another part of the business has successfully delivered the same thing in their domain or the proposer has used the solution elsewhere. Maybe the solution **does** address an issue or a problem in that other circumstance, but can we be sure that our issue here is exactly the same?

When you think about many sales pitches that we encounter along the way at conferences, seminars and the like, they are usually selling you a solution to a problem that you may or may not have. Buy this product, install this system, use this idea.

If you have not assessed the issue or the problem that you are trying to solve before heading off on a change journey, you are likely to solve (or indeed, create) a different problem.

When you turn up in the Emergency Department of a hospital with a massive pain in your abdomen, the medical staff do a whole lot of pushing and prodding to be sure of the problem before they start taking your appendix out. The appendectomy **may** be the right solution, but I'd argue that it's better to be certain of the current state before we proceed with our chosen action.

Only when we know what we are trying to solve, can we start the process.

B is for Brainstorm

So, we now know what it is we are trying to solve.

Here is where the fun should start. Give everyone permission to seriously brainstorm. Not just come up with tried and tested solutions that are predictable and might go some way towards solving our issue.

Go into a room with as many people as you need and declare that there is no such thing as a silly idea. Give people space and time to operate outside of the metaphoric box that our thinking is often constrained by.

Encourage the quiet and less experienced members of your team to put their ideas forward. When you think about it, the more experienced and vocal members of the room will often be the purveyors of the tried and tested. Those whose voices are often ignored will bring forward the ideas that may not have been thought of before.

And if **anyone** says, 'that's a silly idea', eject them from the room immediately.

C is for Consider

If we have done the previous step correctly, there will be lots of ideas and proposed solutions on the table (or more likely, on the whiteboard or the plethora of sticky notes or sheets of butchers' paper attached to the wall).

But before we start our Consideration phase, we need to make sure that we know what success looks like.

Too often we get to the end of a change program and can't really tell whether we have been successful because we didn't spell out what success looks like up front.

Remember what I said about the difference between 'here is a problem we are trying to solve' and 'here is a solution I want you to deliver'. Our success criteria must measure against how well we have eliminated/solved the problem and not how well we have delivered the solution, implemented a system, re-designed an organisation, etc.

Knowing what those success measures are should help us during this Consideration phase. As we go through each of the Brainstormed ideas, we should be able to assess their relative merit by determining how well they will solve our problem or issue, at least at a high level.

There is always a cost consideration as well. But my challenge is always 'what will it cost us to solve this problem' rather than 'what solution can we afford with this budget'.

Yes, there may well have to be a compromise reached that balances these two questions out but whatever we choose to do **must** address the problem we identified during the Assessment phase.

D is for Decide

With our Consideration completed, we should be ready to Decide on our way forward.

Once our Decision is made and endorsed by those who need to endorse it, **then and only then** should we get started on the next phase.

E is for Execute

This is where the traditional Change Management model often kicks in for the first time and, in many cases, this reflects why a change activity doesn't succeed.

If this is the first point at which your change experts have been engaged, they will have missed all of the good stuff performed in Steps A to D and therefore may feel like they are delivering a solution rather than making a change. Get your change people in at **Assess** – they will feel more engaged and you will maximise your chances of successful delivery.

Execute is where many of the traditional Change Management methodologies also commence. Often heavy on process and documentation, these methodologies can often appear to be more important than the outcome.

The hallmark of many change programs seems to have been the development of a set of documents that, once created, sit on the metaphoric shelf and never see the light of day again. Think BIA, think Change Plan, think Comms Plan, think Training Needs Analysis, etc.

My approach is to steer away from the **process** and focus my attention on these questions:

- What is the current state?

- What does the future look like?

- What does successful delivery look like?

- What are the key activities that need to be completed and when?

- Are there any major constraints or other non-negotiables?

- Who needs to know about the change?

- How will this change impact on them?

- What do we need to tell them?

- Who needs to learn new skills or knowledge?

- What are going to be the primary sources of resistance?

- What are the steps we need to take to achieve success?

- How do we make sure that the change 'sticks'?

By taking this approach, we are still focusing on the key elements of change without being hung up on jargon. I'll pick this up in more detail in **Chapter 2**.

Another reason I prefer this approach is that it steers away from an emphasis on documentation and towards answers and activities.

For example, if you ask a Change Manager to talk you through their Business Impact Assessment (BIA), they will often produce a spreadsheet. While this is usually a worthwhile document, the BIA should be an **activity** – an assessment activity – and not just a spreadsheet.

Developing a Communications Plan or a Training Needs Analysis sounds like creating a couple of complex documents. Answering questions 8 and 9 from the list above sounds less daunting and puts an emphasis on the activity rather than the resultant documents.

Just a thought.

F is for Finalise

Is there anything more frustrating than a project that gets 80% delivered and then starts to taper off to nothing?

This typically occurs when a significant amount of the work has been completed and the Project Management Office or someone from the leadership team starts looking towards the next change program.

They start looking at who they can engage on their new project and, rather than actually waiting for the existing project to finish, they start inviting them to meetings for the new piece of work.

Why does this happen?

In my mind, one of the primary reasons relates to not having any clear success criteria defined at the Consideration phase (or even earlier!). If we don't have those success criteria defined, we can't demonstrate whether the project has finished or not. In the absence of a definitive line between 'project still going' and 'project complete', leaders will make their own assessments and act accordingly.

The much better approach is to have a clear set of success criteria and make a deliberate statement of completion. If not all criteria have been met, the project continues. If all criteria **have** been met, the project is Finalised.

G is for GO!

This step is a celebration of success!

Once finalised, the project team and the colleagues who have been impacted should take a step back and reflect on the work they have completed to get to the end successfully.

Maybe you should have a ceremony. Maybe everyone should receive a note of congratulations. Maybe there should be a big red button that someone presses to sound a siren and declare 'GO'.

H is for Handover

Another grey area in change projects is the Handover from the project team to Business As Usual. This step should be formalised after the GO! event and follow an agreed period of hypercare.

Finalise the documentation. Archive the plan. Formally pass

the baton from the project team to the business leaders.

This Handover step ensures that everyone involved knows that the business is now accountable and that the project team have moved onto other activities.

Chapter 2

My Simple Change Plan Template

We have talked a lot about the value of a change plan and how so many of them seemed to be written and very quickly forgotten about.

I have developed a Change Plan template that removes the jargon and complex methodologies associated with a traditional change plan. Instead, it is broken into four parts with a series of questions within each section.

If you answer each of these questions, you'll have a simple, relevant and usable change plan.

It is challenging to include a link to a template in a printed or audio book and so if you would like a copy of the template in a ready-to-use PowerPoint format, please visit the **Change Change** website (**www.changechange.au**) and click on the download link.

Define It

Before kicking off, we need to have a very clear picture of where we are starting and where we intend to end up. Think about a road trip. When you ask your navigation app to plot out the best route to take, it only needs two pieces of information – where you are starting and when you want to end up.

Clearly, the better you can describe both the starting point and the end point, the more accurate the proposed route can be.

What is the current state?

This is one of the most overlooked aspects of developing a change plan. When many change programs kick off, the end state is quite often pre-determined – implement this system, restructure the organisation, etc.

But is the starting point equally well known?

If I tell my GPS that I want to drive to Sydney, I am going to get wildly different proposed routes if I am starting in Brisbane or in Melbourne. In the same way, understanding the starting point of a change plan is key to planning the way forward.

Unfortunately, in many projects and programs, the introduction of a Change Leader only occurs towards the end of the work. This means that the Change Leader often lacks clarity around where the business is starting from – the reason for the change program, the justification for the chosen outcomes, the options that were considered, etc., etc.

If you are the Project or Program Director, please make a conscious decision to include the Change Leader as early as possible. The change plan will be developed within the correct context and from the correct starting point. It will enable the Change Leader to be a part of the decision-making and direction-setting activities.

> **ACTION:** Clearly understand and document the key aspects of the starting point – the why, when and what that has created the need for change.

What does the future state look like?

In my experience, too many change and transformation programs head off with what might be best described as a reasonably clear picture of what the future state might look like. Using my analogy of the drive to Sydney, rather than saying we are heading to 123 The Esplanade in Manly, we set off aiming for the northern suburbs of Sydney.

If you set out for the northern suburbs of Sydney, you'll tick that off as soon as you cross the bridge and drive into North Sydney. Having a specific address like the one in the previous paragraph means that you are close to the end but not quite there yet.

We'll pick this up in the next section but unless you have a clear picture of the finish line, you won't know when you get there.

In many cases, change programs are driven by a timeline and the closest thing some of these programs have to a finishing line is the go-live date and/or the pilot deployment of a system. And so, if we have an unclear starting point and vague end point – it is most unlikely that any documented change plan will be very useful.

> **ACTION:** Document what the future state looks like. Make this as detailed as you can so that anyone who joins the project can understand what you are trying to achieve.

What does successful delivery look like?

How do we know whether we have not only made it to the end but, importantly, how successful we have been in leading our colleagues through the change or transformation?

The only way to sensibly manage this is to have a collection of clearly defined measures that we can assess our change program against.

These measures could be quantitative (e.g. a 5% reduction in operating costs, 90% of phone calls being answered within 10 seconds, etc.) or qualitative (e.g. acceptance of future state by colleagues, enthusiasm for the new ways of working, etc.).

Unless we know what success looks like – before we get started – it is going to be impossible to gauge how well the change plan has worked.

> **ACTION:** Work with the key stakeholders – sponsors, impacted leaders, etc. – to determine how they would like to see the future state and how we can assess it. Waiting until the end of the program to develop success criteria seems counterproductive.

Plan It

What are the key activities that need to be done to complete this change?

Many project plans and change plans that I have seen and have had to work with are documented at such a fine level of granularity they almost implode in on themselves. Thousands and thousands of line items on a project plan, with interdependencies and resource allocations documented.

Don't get me wrong – there is a need for this level of detail, especially when the program is a true transformation program but the change plan is NOT where that detail belongs.

In my world, the change plan needs to contain enough information to enable the Change Leader to be able to explain their approach to colleagues without overwhelming them.

I like to list the key activities and then indicate their expected completion timeline. This document needs to be accessible to anyone impacted by the program and thousands of detailed line items is not going to be helpful in that context.

One of the other key skills required by Change Leaders is the capacity to respond to the unexpected. If this part of the Change Plan is too detailed, responding to the unexpected and maintaining the detailed Change Plan to reflect that response will become onerous. 'Onerous' generally leads to a lack of maintenance and before long, that plan will be the other 'O' word – obsolete.

The Project/Program Director or Project Management Office will clearly need to manage and maintain that detail and you, as the Change Leader will have a role in providing input to that plan. It just doesn't need to be in the Change Plan.

> **ACTION:** List the key activities that need to be successfully completed to deliver the change/transformation. It may be five, it may be ten, it may be twenty or more – only you know how many activities fit the scope of this section of the Change Plan.

Are there any immoveable constraints or not-negotiables?

Like it or not – there will be immovable constraints and there will be not-negotiables that will impact on your capacity to deliver the program outcomes in the way that you think best. I'm not talking about 'that's not what we do around here' …

I'm talking about proper not-negotiables.

Acknowledge them and embrace them. Better still, document them here and get consensus that there is really nothing you can do to get around them. Maybe it's legislation and/or regulation. Maybe there are budgetary constraints. Maybe something else completely.

If they are truly immovable and not negotiable, don't waste time and energy trying to move or negotiate with them.

> **ACTION:** Talk to colleagues, both within the program and external to it. Listen to what they have to say. Discuss and decide whether these hurdles are truly immovable and not negotiable or just hard work to overcome. Either way, bring them out into the open so that time and energy are not wasted.

Who needs to know about the change and how often?

This is traditionally called Stakeholder Engagement and is typically done really well at the start and often fades away. We assemble a list of people who are either directly impacted or otherwise need to know about what we are doing. We might even assign certain stakeholders to key members of the program team to make sure that we give them a briefing when we start.

But what happens after that? Are we **proactively** engaging with the people who need to know?

In many organisations, stakeholder equates to senior colleagues who are decision-makers and need to be aware of any changes we are making. This is certainly a subset of who needs to know, but it is not a comprehensive list.

Let's drop the jargon and the potential for confusing titles like 'stakeholders'. Let's make it easy and refer to the people who need to know what we are up to.

ACTION: Make a list of anyone who needs to know about our change program. This includes people who are directly affected and those who are not specifically impacted but still need to know.

Ensure that you have some kind of schedule for how often you are keeping in touch with each of them.

How will this change impact on them?

You'll notice that I am not calling this a Business Impact Assessment or even a BIA. I am posing this as a question about who is going to be impacted.

Remembering my observation earlier that one size **does not** fit all, think about how you will address the impact on your colleagues. For many, a BIA (deliberate use of the acronym there) results in a spreadsheet that has green, yellow and red cells representing the likely degree of impact but does it address: **How individuals may be impacted differently?**

What we need to do to acknowledge the impact on each individual and how we can minimise/mitigate that impact without diminishing the level of change required?

ACTION: Identify everyone who will be impacted by the change and HOW they will be impacted, not just HOW MUCH. Where roles are impacted in a similar way (e.g. all call centre staff need to follow a different process), group these impacts together BUT be aware that as people, they will feel impact differently.

What do we need to tell them?

We have spoken elsewhere about the difference between communication and engagement. In most change plans, there is a link to a 'Comms Plan' which, more often than not, talks about **who** and **when** various impacted colleagues should receive messages more so than **what** the messaging is.

At this point, I would encourage you to develop the key messages that outline what, where, when and how things will be different, so that all colleagues who engage with others – inside and external to the program – are being consistent.

By all means include a link to an engagement schedule. That engagement schedule should closely reflect the 'who needs to know' document we discussed a couple of sections back.

ACTION: Develop a set of key messages that everyone can use whenever they are engaging with others. The scheduling of any communications activities should be seen as part of the engagement schedule we spoke about earlier.

Who needs to learn new skills or knowledge?

Traditionally known as a Training Needs Analysis, I tend to focus on who needs to know new skills or gain additional knowledge. A Training Needs Analysis tends to focus on who needs to attend a training program – typically in the week before go-live – which I find too restrictive to answer this important question.

New skills and knowledge are not only gained by undertaking a training program. Much of the contextual knowledge should be delivered during the duration of the change program via town hall updates, regular engagement activities, etc. Training programs are typically related to developing new skills (how to use a system, what process to follow, etc.). Knowledge transfer via brain dump is not an effective way to bring impacted colleagues up to speed.

> **ACTION:** Identify everyone who needs to learn new things (skills and knowledge) as early in the process as possible. This allows for the drip feed of knowledge along the way and minimises the likelihood of a brain dump at the end.

Who or what are going to be the likely sources of resistance?

Like it or not, resistance is inevitable. So many change plans I have read pay scant, if any, attention to the likelihood that some impacted colleagues and others will push back and maintain the corporate inertia we have discussed elsewhere.

Identifying the likely sources of resistance proactively – and early – provides you with the best opportunity to develop a strategy to address that resistance and to deliver on that strategy.

Generally, people are not going to resist for the sake of resistance. They usually have genuine concerns or fears that the way forward is not going to work for them. Often – not always – identifying these likely sources of resistance and engaging with them throughout the program leads to clarity, transparency and context, allowing them to see a bigger picture.

And note, that I didn't say communicating to them. I said, engaging with them. Give them the chance to speak, listen to what they have to say and where you can, make allowances. Change and transformation is hard enough without having active resistance. Doing what you can to minimise it is a win for everyone.

ACTION: As you and your colleagues engage with those people who need to know what is going on, listen to the resistors, look for red flags and address them as soon as you can. This might mean a difficult conversation where you acknowledge the resistor's concerns without being able to resolve them. Knowing what you are up against is so much better than having to deal with resistance that you haven't identified.

Do It

So we have defined our change and we have planned our approach. The time has come to deliver. Documenting all of what we have outlined above means you have a change approach that is high in useful content and low on the stuff that often appears in change plans and yet adds little value.

It's time to deliver in our **Do It** phase.

What are key dates to have each step completed?

The Project/Program Director will maintain a highly detailed project plan that outlines tasks, dependencies, constraints and, of course, completion dates.

We don't need that level of detail in our simplified Change Plan. What we do need, however, is a list of the things the Change Team is accountable for delivering and when they need to be completed.

Sure, the timelines on these activities need to reflect the overall timelines and schedules but, in this context, we are only required to list the big-ticket items and when they are due for completion.

Too much detail in this document means much more maintenance and is probably replicating the work of the Project/Program Director and/or the PMO. Keep it simple and keep it focused.

> **ACTION:** Make a list of the things you (and your team, if you have one) are accountable for delivering. The level of detail is your call but, please err on the side of less detail rather than more to avoid wasted energy in maintenance as things inevitably change.

What fine-tuning and refinement will be required as we progress through the Do It phase?

Regardless of how much thinking and planning you

complete upfront, we all know that things will change – unexpected delays, a lack of colleague availability, additional people impacted than first thought etc.

We know it will happen and yet, we don't always factor in maintenance of the change plan during the **Do It** phase. If you don't include a specific activity to review what you created at the start of the journey, the content will become outdated and, as a direct result, irrelevant to what you are doing.

When you have a weekly meeting with your Change team, work through this pack to determine whether things are as they were the last time you revised the document. If you are a solo Change Leader (as many of you will be), put aside a scheduled hour per week to review, revise and update your Change Plan.

ACTION: Diarise a review/revision session every week to ensure that your Change Plan is changing to reflect the inevitable, yet unpredictable, change that will happen. And if there are changes, make sure that you are sharing/collaborating with the other leaders in your Change team.

Make It Stick

How do we make sure that change is embedded in the day-to-day business activities once we complete the change?

I don't know about you but one thing I have noticed as a Change Leader for the past few decades is how often change practitioners are moved onto a different project or, if they are a contractor or consultant, moved out of the organisation, before the project is fully embedded.

If you are lucky, you'll be kept on the project/program until at least the go-live date before being moved sideways or out. But this very rarely includes being around long enough to make sure that the change has been fully accepted and fully embedded into the 'Business As Usual' (BAU) model.

Without that drive from you as the Change Leader, how confident are you that the change will 'stick'? If you were to move away and then come back in six months' time, how confident are you that the changes you led would be still in place or would things have somehow reverted to a hybrid model that lands somewhere between the old and the new.

Developing embedding strategies at the earliest possible

point in the project has a number of advantages:

- It gives a clear statement of what you believe needs to be done to not only deliver the change but also to make it stick.

- It provides some input to 'what successful delivery looks like'.

- It gives you a chance to socialise your proposed embedding strategies with impacted colleagues and to work through any concerns, ideas and suggestions that your colleagues may provide.

- It gives the BAU teams a list of things to complete in the event that you are moved on from your involvement before the program is fully embedded.

ACTION: Think about the things that you – or the 'Business As Usual' team – can do to ensure that impacted colleagues don't slip back into bad habits and the old way of doing things. Document them and socialise them early so that everyone has the chance to review and revise them well before they are needed.

Chapter 3
Transformation

Now let's consider my definition of transformation.

Transformation is about changing something completely – changing its function, making it operate or exist in a totally different way.

The prefix 'trans' comes from the Latin for 'across' or 'beyond'. The second part of the word – formation – relates to how things are arranged or set out.

The word transformation, therefore, tells us that we are doing something that takes us beyond our current state. We are not staying with the current or existing formation. Transformation is literally an activity that takes us beyond where we currently exist.

Do you see the distinction between change and transformation? Many people seem to think that transformation is simply a 'big change' and I can see a degree of logic in that thinking.

But – **and it is a big but** – transformation also requires making something different in function, in operation, in its appearance or … here's the kicker … exist in a totally different way.

Let's revisit our example from the first chapter – the change being made by painting the wall of a meeting room green. We agreed (didn't we?) that this was a change because the end result was different to how we started out.

But, when the change is complete, the room is still a meeting room. You probably book it the same way as you used to. Yes, it has a green wall but otherwise it is still the same meeting room as it always was.

If we want to **transform** the meeting room, we need to end up with something that 'exists in a totally different way'. The meeting room might now be a café or a staff breakout area. It may now be a production studio because we have deployed some new technology into the space and created superior acoustics.

Now, we are talking transformation.

Transformation cannot be accidental. Sure, it may be caused by something unexpected, but when all is said and done, someone needs to have a vision of what the future state looks like and set out deliberately to achieve that future state.

So while transformation involves a big change, big change is not necessarily a transformation. Typically change takes place as the result of a project whereas transformation normally needs a program of work to be delivered successfully.

Change is often reactive – this has happened and so, we need to react. Transformation is very rarely reactive – it is planned, intentional and deliberate.

How Well Is Your Business Operating?

This is a really important question to ask before we go too much further.

I want you to be totally honest here. I am not going to make you write it down or say it out loud. Just answer the question to yourself.

I should give credit here to Melbourne radio legend, Ross Stevenson, who developed a very similar approach to rating things. He has given me permission to adapt his model and use it here in my book.

Here we go …

If 0 equals 'my business is completely off the rails' and 100 equals 'my business could not be running any better', give your business a score of between 0 and 100, but not using a number that is a multiple of 5.

I'll repeat the question – how well is your business running, 0 to 100, no multiples of 5?

If you have given your business a score between 90 and 100, you don't need to read any further into this book. I think we would all be pretty happy with a business that is running that well (assuming that you have been totally honest, of course).

If you have given your business a score that is greater than, let's say, 75, I'd say you have a few **changes** to make and hopefully, you have picked up some ideas in the previous sections.

If you have given yourself a score that is between 50 and 75, I think you need to seriously consider a program of **transformation**. Change isn't enough to bring your operational score up to where it needs to be. Some tough decisions are needed.

If your score lands between 25 and 50, I can't wait for you to get to the next main section of the book – **Transformagination®**. More about that later.

And if you have scored between 0 and 25 … mmm … I'm really not sure what to suggest.

Newton's First and Second Laws of Business

Isaac Newton was one of the greatest physicists of all time – in fact, many sources suggest that he is in the top 10 of the most influential people in history.

Despite suggestions to the contrary, he didn't actually **discover** gravity (I think people might have had an inkling before he was born that, when you let go of something, it drops to the ground). Instead, he developed the theory that helps to **explain** gravity.

Likewise, he developed three laws of motion, two of which are very applicable here. I like to refer to them as Newton's First and Second Laws of Business.

In the context of motion, the first law goes a bit like this – a body will keep moving at the same speed and in the same direction (or, as physicists like to say, at the same velocity) until and unless an external force is applied. This includes an item standing still until a force is applied to make it start moving.

In an excellent marketing strategy, Newton took his first law (the one I have just described) and created his second law by pretty much saying the same thing in a different way. His second law states that the degree of change in the velocity – that is, the acceleration – is directly proportional to that force. The bigger the external force, the bigger the impact on the body.

Let's apply this to your business for a moment. If your business is like the vast majority of businesses and other organisations that I have dealt with over the years, you will typically operate today like you did yesterday and the day before and last week. Likewise, you'll probably do it all the same way again tomorrow.

Unless you apply some degree of external force, things will keep sailing along as they have been – in the same direction and at the same speed.

We can apply a small force – maybe adjust a process here and there – but at the end of the day, a small force will equate to a small change and you're probably not a whole lot better off.

To **transform** your business, however, you are going to need a bigger external force. A deliberate effort. An intentional and significant intervention.

Remember, transformation is defined as 'changing something completely – changing its function, making it operate or exist in a totally different way'. If you are serious about transformation, you'd better read the next section.

Transformation Is Never An Accident

We have already discussed the difference between **change** and **transformation**. But here are a few specifics around that difference.

Change can be minor. Transformation can NOT be minor. If an action or a series of actions is going to fundamentally change the function or appearance of something (that is, transform it), then there will need to be significant and intentional effort imposed.

Change can occur with little momentum. Transformation needs a champion – sometimes a superhero – to drive it, often against strong tides of organisational inertia.

Change is a process. Transformation is more of a mindset, an attitude.

True transformation creates discomfort. True

transformation creates uncertainty. True transformation creates disruption.

Change often happens by accident.

Transformation is never an accident. Transformation is always a deliberate choice.

Same Old, Same Old …

There's a phrase that gets me fired up. Closely related to 'same s**t, different day' (tidied up for family viewing), no one ever uses either phrase to inspire themselves or anyone around them, do they?

You ask someone how they are and there it is … same old, same old. Ask them how their day is going … same s**t, different day.

To me, both phrases translate to much the same thing – a statement of acceptance of their mediocre circumstances. It says to me, 'I am just going through the motions and can't be bothered doing anything to change it'.

Well, here's a tip. If you do nothing about changing your circumstances today, you will more than likely find yourself in exactly the same place tomorrow. Sure, you might win the lottery later today (which will undoubtedly change your circumstances!), but given the very low likelihood of that happening, the only other way that things will change is if YOU take specific and intentional action.

And that's just to invoke change – if we are talking about transformation (and we are!), that specific and intentional action needs to be significant.

Here are a few ideas.

Decide if you want things to be different.

Maybe you are happy doing what you're doing, being where you are, going through the 'same old, same old' motions. If that's the case, that's fine – just invent a new phrase that doesn't sound so defeatist. Please.

Talk to people about how you want things to transform.

If you are uncertain about what steps to take to transform your business or your circumstances, talk to somebody you trust, somebody who has been through a similar process, someone who inspires you. If you genuinely want to improve yourself or your circumstances, most people will give you their time for a chat.

Take active steps to transform.

There are plenty of cliches about standing still (if you aren't moving forward, you're moving backwards, etc.) and there is some truth in each of them. As Albert Einstein said (and I am almost certainly paraphrasing the great man):

> **'If you always do what you've always done,**
> **you'll always get what you've always got.'**

As mentioned earlier, another great physicist, Isaac Newton, alluded to something similar in one of his laws of motion but which is just as relevant in other aspects of life:

> **'An object at rest stays at rest and an object**
> **in motion stays in motion with the same speed**
> **and in the same direction unless acted upon by**
> **an unbalanced force.'**

In other words, if no external force is applied to something, it won't change.

Being someone who likes to think in a logical way, it appears to me that there are only two options available – (1) keep on doing what you always have and get the 'same old, same old' outcomes OR (2) do something that creates a transformation.

It's obviously your call but I'm very keen on the second option. That said, remember that the second option is about action and it is about transformation … action and transformation that YOU have to drive.

Engagement vs Communication

This is such an important distinction and yet, one that so many businesses fail to acknowledge. How many of you reading this are considered to be 'change and comms' experts? Rarely do we see this role described as it should be – Engagement and Change.

Let's firstly look at how Communications teams often work in businesses and other organisations.

A 'comms plan' is usually developed early in the project lifecycle, often because the program manager says that you need one. More often than not, it consists of 'key messages' or 'scripts', various audience groups and a schedule. If you like, it more or less translates into 'who needs to know what, when?'

In almost every case, the proposed comms are one-way, same-way messages, quoting those scripts that everyone has agreed on and, more often than not, presented as emails to impacted colleagues.

As I mentioned earlier, my take on this type of communication is like printing a whole stack of identical brochures and throwing them over the fence, hoping someone will pick one up and read it.

And in the case of a minor change program (remember our green wall?), that might be enough to get the message out to the masses.

But let's consider how successful this might be in a transformation.

For starters, we have already agreed that transformation is significantly different to a change activity because transformation is about changing something completely – changing its function, making it operate or exist in a totally different way. This says to me that sending out messages and hoping someone reads them is just not going to cut it.

So, how does engagement differ from communication?

In the strict definition of each word, you might be forgiven for thinking that are both are two-way interactions between parties.

But think about the most recent change or transformation program you went through. Can you honestly say that the communication was two-way? That the recipients of the messaging were able to have a two-way interaction?

Now think about the word engagement. In just about every context I can think of, engagement is, by definition, a relationship-based interaction. Ongoing. Equal on both sides. Neither party being more important than the other.

Sure, communication is a very important part of engagement but rather than being simply transactional, engagement means creating a relationship that is mutually beneficial.

Think about a transformation program you have been through. You may have even been a part of the transformation team.

When something is fundamentally changing its function and operating in a totally different way to how it operated before, I don't want people just telling me what is happening. I want to be a part of the transformation. I want to learn about what the transformation is going to deliver and how I will be impacted. I want an opportunity to develop a relationship where I feel empowered to ask questions and make suggestions – the sorts of things that the one-way stuff doesn't allow.

Can transformation be successful with communication only or does it require engagement? Based on what I have just said, it seems to me to be a no-brainer.

Chapter 4

Transformagination®

We are going to unpack **Transformagination**® very soon but let's kick around a couple of other very important concepts first.

Imagine

In 1971, John Lennon challenged us to **imagine**.

What a wonderful, powerfully liberating word that is.

Imagine.

When you imagine, anything is possible. You are no longer constrained by what seems to be a series of limits that are based on experience, rules and other hurdles to creativity and innovation.

These constraints seem to be something that we learn and

develop as we get older and, dare I say it, more cynical.

When I was four years old, Superman was my hero. We are talking about the black and white TV show, filmed in the 1950s and featuring George Reeves as Superman. No special effects beyond some clever cinematography that made George look like he was flying but, in reality, was laying on a table or suspended by wires to give that impression.

It didn't stop me thinking that maybe other people could fly – like me! I have a scar on my right hand to remind me that little boys can't fly and, if you are trying, not to do so near sharp galvanised iron sheeting.

I **imagined** I could fly. No limits. No learned apprehension.

Another man who influenced me along the way was Albert Einstein. Let the record show that he was an exceptional mathematician and physicist. Despite four years at one of Australia's leading Schools of Physics, I still struggle to understand the physics and mathematics he told us about at anything more than a very, very basic level.

But he was more than a physicist and mathematician. He was one of the greatest philosophers in history. A man of theories and deep thinking.

Don't believe me? Do a quick online search for 'Einstein

Quotes' and see how you go. There are many websites specifically dedicated to Einstein quotes.

One of my favourites is this, taken from a 1929 interview with the Saturday Evening Post (published in Philadelphia, USA):

'Imagination is more important than knowledge.'

I had a poster on my bedroom wall throughout my teenage years with Einstein's photo and that quote written underneath.

I ended up teaching mathematics and physics to secondary school students here in Victoria, Australia – two subjects that are not generally associated with imagination. They tend to be exact sciences that may, on the face of it, seem to exist to provide only two kinds of answer – right and wrong.

And yet, the great man demonstrated that unless you had a great imagination, you were destined to do the same thing over and over again.

So, what is Transformagination®?

Transformagination® is a concept that I have developed

and written about since 2019.

It is obviously a *portmanteau* (two words coming together to form a new word) of **transformation** and **imagination**. It is the bringing together the concepts of totally changing the function or appearance of something (transformation) without the constraints that would otherwise exist (imagination).

Picking up on our previous example of the meeting room:

Change is when we paint the wall green – it is still a meeting room but the wall is a different colour.

Transformation is when we convert the existing room into a café or production studio.

Transformagination® is what happens when we start from scratch. There is a totally blank canvas to work with. Words like 'suppose' and 'imagine' tend to get used when we start thinking **transformaginatively**.

And yes, thinking **transformaginatively** may take you to a place that you feel is impossible to achieve now or in the short-to-medium term future. I am not saying that, by coming up with a **transformaginative** idea, you will be able to implement it straight away.

That's not the point of **Transformagination**®.

Transformagination® means pushing the conventional boundaries of strategic thinking. It is challenging people to get well outside of their comfort zone. It is coming up with **really** creative ideas and then seeing how close you can get to making them happen.

In fact, if you come up with what you believe is a **transformaginative** idea but one that you can implement in the short to medium term, maybe, just maybe, you haven't pushed the boundaries far enough!

We're going to talk more about what this looks like in the pages that follow. Buckle up, settle in and let's start **transformagining**.

Think outside of the box ... what box?

How often do you hear workshop presenters or facilitators encouraging participants to **really think outside the box**. I guess it's their best attempt to have the workshop participants trying to come up with some fresh ideas.

But you're heard the old idiom – **everything old is new again**. And the other old idiom **the more things change, the more they stay the same**.

Transformaginists don't subscribe to either of these idioms.

We also reject the concept of 'thinking outside of the box'.

Why?

Because in our **transformaginative** world, **there is no box**. Having a box to think outside of suggests that we are acknowledging that there are some constraints that we have considered and then step past them.

Transformagination® says 'what box … there is no box'.

Let go. Forget that there was ever a box and start imagining.

There are no limits

Closely related to the previous observation, a **transformaginative** thinker will think beyond any self-imposed or, indeed, business-imposed limits.

When I was a small child, the concept of 'the sky's the limit' was arguably a valid point. I was given a book called 'You Will Go To The Moon' by Mae and Ira Freeman and illustrated by Robert Patterson. I still have the book – in fact, it is sitting on my desk in front of me as I write this section. The book was first published in 1959 – a book that was literally, in those days, science fiction.

Then, on 20 July 1969, a couple of Americans – Neil Armstrong and Edwin 'Buzz' Aldrin – actually set foot on the moon, showing that not even the sky was the limit. Since then, of course, other space probes have gone even further to the far reaches of our solar system.

I want to challenge the idea that the sky is the limit. Armstrong and Aldrin certainly did not see the sky as the limit nor did anyone who followed them to the moon, on space shuttles or space stations. Mae and Ira Freeman certainly didn't think that the sky was the limit either.

Think about your business with a mindset that there are no limits. None. Imagine your business being whatever you want it to be and strive towards being that business.

I know what you are thinking. That is an unrealistic way to plan your business and I get that. I have been working in the corporate world since 1989 and understand that there are constraints that will undoubtedly stop you or at least slow you down as you strive towards that **transformagined** business.

But don't let that inevitability get in the way of your imagination. Dream big. Dream unrealistically. Dream **transformaginatively**.

And you just never know what you might achieve.

By the way, I have just gone looking for 'You Will Go To

The Moon' online. Used copies are selling through a global bookseller for anywhere between AU$70 and AU$300. I'm glad I still have mine!

The Window Conundrum

Consider a log cabin with three solid walls and a fourth wall that contains a single window. That window is perfectly square – from top to bottom, the window measures exactly 1 metre. From left to right, the window measures exactly 1 metre.

Can you picture it?

So now I get my power saw and make the window exactly twice as big as it was before. I now have three solid walls and the same fourth wall, still with a single window, but now that window is twice the size it was before. And it is still square AND it is still 1 metre top to bottom and 1 metre left to right.

That simply can't be possible … can it?

Well, conventional thinking says it's impossible. But, as you know, we think conventional thinking is SO overrated. What would a **transformaginative** thinker make of this?

We're not going to tell you how this is possible and if you've worked it out, we'd love it if you didn't spill the beans either.

Somewhere else in this book you will find the answer to this conundrum – I'm not going to tell you where. All I will tell you is that it requires some real imagination and a complete departure from conventional thinking.

Good luck!

Are you spending too much time looking behind you?

I assume that as a reader of this book you have driven a car or a motorcycle – even ridden a bike.

There is a lesson here to help you as you develop a **transformaginative** mindset.

Let's talk about driving a car but this observation is equally applicable to bikes, motorcycles or any other vehicle.

I drive a medium-sized SUV which according to the specifications has a front windscreen and three rear vision mirrors. The total area of the front windscreen is around 25 times bigger than the cumulative total area of the three rear vision mirrors. This doesn't consider the size of the side windows that also allow me to see even more of what's ahead of me rather than what's behind me.

In business, we tend to spend a lot of time looking behind

us and not enough looking forward. We have end-of-month reviews, we pore over spreadsheets looking at trends based on last month and last quarter and even this time last year.

I am not saying that there is no value in looking back but – are we spending enough time looking forward?

Setting future strategies that are **transformaginative** rely on letting go of the past. By all means use it as a reference point and as a driver to do things very differently.

But don't spend too much time looking back. You might drive past the exit … or worse.

Being the Chief 'No Risk' Officer

Most large corporate organisations have a Chief Risk Officer (CRO) – either someone with that title or someone who takes on the responsibility for risk management across the business.

But I have a theory that we should rename them the Chief No-Risk Officer.

In my corporate experience, many projects are worked and re-worked until most, if not all, of the risk is eliminated, well before the proposal gets anywhere near the Chief Risk Officer.

How often do you think a proposal lands on the CRO's desk that causes them to say, 'You want to do what?' or 'Are you serious? I think we'd better work through some options'?

I think the answer is either (a) never or (b) very, very rarely. Reports, proposals and ideas are generally revised, consolidated and heavily sanitised on their way to final approval. By the time the CRO sees any proposal, there is a significant likelihood that there will be very little, if any, risk to be considered.

I worked in an organisation a few years ago that had three levels of risk assessment before anything went to the CRO for approval. That translates to:

Are you sure? Yes

Are you really sure? Yes

Are you really, really sure? Yes

Okay, then let's send it off to the CRO so that we can be really, really, REALLY sure.

In the world of **Transformagination**®, we are not constrained in our thinking. There are no limits to the possibilities. In our world, the Chief No-Risk Officer SHOULD be challenged. They SHOULD be made to wonder whether the proposal is too risky.

Change typically brings some risk and some reward. Transformation brings more risk but should deliver more reward. It goes without saying, then, that **Transformagination**® brings even more risk but is where the biggest rewards are on offer. Bold and brave decisions need to be made. Program teams must consist of dedicated people who are clear on the risk but committed to delivering the outcomes.

That doesn't mean that **Transformagination**® is applicable in all organisations in all circumstances. It doesn't mean that **Transformagination**® ignores risk. It certainly doesn't mean that you can barge through with no regard to what might happen if things go wrong. Sensible and rational thinking is also a key component of **Transformagination**®.

But it does mean that every Chief Risk Officer will need to be on their game!

Could vs Should

There is only a subtle difference between the spelling of these two words but a profound difference when developing a strategic plan.

Change and transformation generally involve SHOULD.

Undoubtedly, **Transformagination**® needs to involve COULD.

I have spoken to a number of businesses who, when developing their five-year plan or undertaking some other form of strategic activity, place an enormous emphasis on the word SHOULD. Next year, we SHOULD change our processes, we SHOULD allow hybrid working, we SHOULD broaden our product range, we SHOULD review the way we operate, etc., etc.

All of these are valid things to consider but what if we introduced a new **Transformaginative** dimension to our thinking? How about we focus on what we COULD achieve. We COULD totally transform the way we do business. We COULD introduce new services. We COULD …

SHOULD implies adherence to some rules, standards, expectations, behaviours or directives. COULD implies total creativity, transformation and, as you know, one of my favourite words – imagination. SHOULD means keeping one eye on the past and making decisions accordingly. COULD means doing things in a totally new way.

No limits. No heritage. No legacy.

As I have said throughout, **Transformagination**® is not for everyone nor for every business. That said, dismissing it out of hand because of what you SHOULD do is ignoring the extraordinary things you COULD do with some effort and imagination.

The dreaded apostrophe

I remember going to a training session many years ago which included a presentation from Dr Paul Callery, an exercise scientist and former VFL (now AFL) player with over 180 games with Melbourne, St Kilda and South Melbourne (now Sydney Swans).

At 165cm, Paul was one of the shortest players to ever play the game at the elite level and based his approach to football on the fact that, during his youth, he was often told what he 'can't' do because of his stature. His point was that if you drop the **'t** from **can't** it becomes **can**.

This is very much along the same lines as **Should** vs **Could**, isn't it?

A **Transformaginist** will always favour **could** over **should** and likewise, will always have a bias towards **can** rather than **can't**, **do** rather than **don't**, **will** rather than **won't**.

In fact, when you think about it, there are not many contractions (that is, an abbreviated word that contains an apostrophe) that have a positive connotation, are there? Apart from the ones I have listed in the previous paragraph, there are several that have a level of regret about them – could've, should've, might've, would've, couldn't, should've … you get the picture.

Apostrophes, on the whole, are a major speed bump in the art of **Transformagination®**. There will be times where the apostrophe is required and where some of those contractions are necessary. But please don't use them when the creative juices are flowing. Please don't say 'that can't ever happen' or 'we won't be able to achieve that'.

Let the ideas flow and, rather than discussing what you **can't** achieve, focus on what you **can**. Rather than dwelling on why something **couldn't** happen, develop strategies on why it **could**.

Yes, it is a significant mindset shift but one that is liberating and, to be totally honest, lots of fun.

Learning to swim … while holding the side of the swimming pool

Picture this. You decide that you want to learn to swim. You head down to the local swimming pool and the instructor tells you that, to be safe, you are going to learn to swim by holding onto the side of the pool. That way, if things go wrong, you can always climb out of the pool.

That's just plain silly, isn't it? At some point, if you want to learn to swim, you are going to have to leave the side of the pool and remove the safety net of being able to reach out and grab the ladder. Sure, there are steps you need to take and knowledge you need to gain before letting go but if you are ever going to learn to swim, you'll need to just let go and give it a crack.

Bring that analogy into your next planning workshop. If you are always going to have one hand holding onto the side of the metaphoric swimming pool, are you ever going to be able to REALLY let go and **transformaginate**?

You need to take the plunge/dive off the high board/jump in at the deep end (I've run out of pool analogies!). If you are serious about doing things differently, you'll only make tiny little baby steps if you continue to cling to the safety rail.

The problem is …

It would have been more than 15 years ago. I was working on a transformation program that, among other things, was looking to move the organisation's financial services from a federated model to a centralised model.

Yes, this meant that people would be impacted. Processes and reporting would need to change. Effort would be needed, especially around the changeover date.

We employed an engagement approach rather than a simple communications model (see the earlier section called **Engagement vs Communication** if you are unsure of the difference).

One of the key players was a colleague who had worked within the organisation for well over 20 years. She was seen as the main subject matter expert and, sadly, was the primary source of resistance to what we were trying to achieve.

And yet, 15 years later, that meeting sits clearly in my memory for one significant reason. Within the space of 30 minutes, that colleague had used the phrase 'the problem is' at least 20 times.

There was no effort on her part to work with us to create something new. Every time we proposed a new way of doing something it was met with 'yes, but the problem is *insert an appropriate reason for saying the problem is*'.

It didn't matter what we said, she had a counter argument always prefaced with the same few words.

There is no place for 'the problem is' in a **Transformagination**® activity. The naysayers are going to slow you down and never let you get to a point where 'could' becomes the key word in the conversation.

Recognise that **Transformagination**® is tough for some people, especially those who feel that the conversation is going to places where their role or power base is under threat. This colleague was going to change from being the longest serving person under the existing structure to being the same as everyone else under the new structure.

I spent some time with her after that fateful 30-minute meeting. She agreed that she was reacting out of fear rather than participating in shaping the way forward.

Why do I tell this story? There are a few reasons:

- Engagement works so much better than communication. Imagine if we had not taken the time to sit with her, to listen to what she had to say and to work with her, through to the acceptance of the new model.

- When creating a **Transformagination**® session, think about who you want to have in that workshop. That doesn't mean that you should exclude people from the overall process. It means that when you are seriously **transformagining**, you are better served to have people who won't slow you down with phrases like 'the problem is'.

- Not everyone can **transformaginate**. Just like not everyone can sing, dance or cook well. If people don't want to be part of the session, thank them for being honest and move on without them. That said, of course, when the **transformagining** session has been done and decisions have been made, make sure you double back and include them via a transparent engagement plan.

Being an oldie

Being an oldie myself (certainly in a work/career sense), I feel that I can comment about this without too much prejudice.

Think about the people who are in control of most large corporate organisations. Most are in the second half of their careers, a significant proportion of them are males who have spent their entire career working their way through their particular industry or sector and have arrived at what they probably think is the pinnacle of their career.

You can understand the thinking behind why these people are running organisations. They have 'been there, done that'. They have just about seen everything there is to see within their industry. They know which levers to pull when a particular crisis arises because they have done it before and they have seen their solution work.

All of that works brilliantly – unless you want to actually want to **transformaginate**.

Transformagination® is, by definition, about thinking in totally new ways. What COULD happen if we imagined.

How much of a restriction does 30 or 40 years in the same industry, being reliable, being predictable, reducing risk, etc. create when trying to imagine what COULD be done.

No, my feeling is that if we are truly going to take on **Transformagination**®, we need to **actively** involve the young, the inexperienced and the new-to-industry people within our organisation. They are the ones who bring fresh, unrestricted thoughts to the table. They are the ones whose imagination is less likely to be coloured by their career to date.

I am not, for one minute, saying that the strategic direction of your organisation should be handed over to the less experienced colleagues within your business.

What I am saying is that, if you really want to push the

boundaries, to get fresh ideas of what your organisation COULD do or be, to really think **transformaginally**, it's not going to happen with a room full of 50+ year old executives.

Also, if you are going to invite some of the 'young ones' along, make sure that you give them space to contribute. Imagine yourself all those years ago in a room full of senior leaders and executives. As a less experienced participant, they will probably feel intimidated and reticent to say much unless you actively encourage them to.

They are there for a reason so give them an opportunity to speak and to be heard. This is sometimes where the magic appears.

As Einstein said (paraphrasing loosely) – if you always do what you have always done, you'll always get what you have always got. Another way of saying the same thing is this – if you always listen to the same people, you'll probably hear the same thing.

And as you have probably worked out by now, **Transformagination**® can only, and will only, occur where new, creative and fresh ideas are given airtime – and are listened to.

The Power Base Removal

I have already written about how some people are resistant to change, regardless of how well the change is explained to them. So why is that?

I think that it often stems from the removal of an individual's power base.

Everyone secretly loves being powerful in some way or another – being the one who has been in the department for the longest, the one who holds the division's procurement card, the person who books the flights and accommodation for the team … you know who and what I mean.

If you introduce change – moving a colleague to a new department in a restructure, giving everyone a P-card, giving all colleagues the authority to book their own travel, etc. – this erodes the power base of those impacted.

This is worth considering whenever you deliver change or transformation programs. In this section, though, we are talking about **Transformagination**® … so, why is it relevant?

In my mind, it is even **more** relevant when we are **transformagining**. If we are doing it right, the people who normally make the decisions are going to have **their** power base removed – something they won't be used to and are very likely to push back on.

Most organisations have a traditional structure where the most experienced people are sitting at the top of the organisational chart, making the decisions and setting the strategy. If we are **really serious** about **transformagining**, those people need to take a step back and allow the truly creative, truly innovative people – typically the less experienced, more inclined to think outside of the organisational heritage – to take the reins.

Remove the legacy thinking that is usually brought to the table by the most experienced (and very often, the least flexible) colleagues and replace it with innovative and creative thinking, led by the people who have traditionally been ignored when setting strategy.

That's going to take some brave thinking – and some courageous behaviour – across the entire organisation. People who have traditionally led the strategic planning and thinking, taking a step back and allowing those who traditionally haven't, to have their day.

Are you ready to be truly innovative?

Innovation isn't what it used to be

Earlier, I wrote that I think that the definition of transformation has been watered down over time. The word was always used in its truest sense – changing something completely, changing its function, making it operate or exist in a totally different way.

My recent observation is that project leaders have started describing large change projects as transformations when in fact they are just big changes. Is that so that it sounds more impressive on their resume? Maybe.

But the same thing seems to have happened to the word **innovation**. Innovation, to me, is the development of totally new ideas with the emphasis on **totally new.** Innovation goes hand in hand with creativity and, often, risk. It is about stepping outside of the tried and true and into a world where you are leading the way.

Job descriptions for Change Managers often talk about 'implementing new and innovative solutions to the business' when, in fact, all the project is really doing is more of the same, implementing something that one or more of their competitors have already done for their customers.

To me, when music stopped being delivered via records

(easy to scratch) and cassettes (easy to stretch) and started arriving on CDs, that was an innovation. When that music was delivered digitally, that was innovation, too. When cars started adding airbags that opened on impact, that was an innovation. When babies could be conceived via IVF, that was an innovation.

Taking an idea that worked in one division of your organisation and applying it to another division is leveraging an idea. Not innovating. Changing the packaging of a product is not an innovation – it is changing the packaging.

Innovation plays on **Transformagination®'s** home ground. People who have truly innovated have been **transformaginists**, probably even without realising. Some of these ideas required people to think far and away beyond what their organisation had traditionally encouraged.

Innovation requires a totally new way of thinking. It requires bravery. It requires vision. It requires space. It requires risk-taking. It requires imagination.

If any of these things are missing, you are probably not going to get innovation.

Neither is disruption

Remember when calling yourself a **disruptor** was all the rage?

We have seen true disruptors and the impact they have had on their industry sector has been profound. Think Amazon. Think Uber. Think Apple. In each case, they were **transformaginists** without even knowing it.

As is the case with innovation, there seems to be a high level of tolerance around people who claim to be disruptors. Setting up an online store to rival Amazon is not being a disruptor. Creating a new ridesharing app to rival Uber is not being a disruptor.

Disruption is being radical. Disruption is about fundamentally transforming a business or sector such that things will never be the same again.

When the local grocer was replaced by a supermarket – that was disruption. When digital photography was introduced – that was disruption. When Henry Ford introduced the assembly line and, with it, mass production – that was disruption.

And when you think about it, every one of these ideas had

several factors in common – radical thinking, an ability to imagine, a preparedness to take risks, a willingness to try and fail, a capacity to not just think outside of the box but to get rid of the box, to imagine what **could** happen not just **should**.

Ringing any bells?

Be de-constructive to be constructive

Tied in with our swimming pool analogy a few pages back, where we spoke about having to let go of the side of the pool to learn to swim, we also need to acknowledge that sometimes the best renovations involve knocking down part or all of the existing structure.

If you are committed to maintaining an existing structure, your ability to renovate is limited. If the structure stays, you can paint the walls and lay new carpet but that's about it. Knock down a few walls and suddenly the scope for change – in fact, for transformation – is significantly enhanced.

If we are thinking **Transformagination®**, the need to deconstruct is absolutely required before we even get to construction.

There is that old saying that you have to break a few eggs

to make an omelette. I'm taking that and re-using it – you'll need to knock the old building down if you want to **Transformaginate**.

I am, of course, speaking figuratively here. We are not going to pull a building down and then start the process of **Transformagination**®.

As I have said elsewhere, **Transformagination**® is a mindset. Imagine that the building **had** been knocked down. How would we approach the rebuild without any pre-existing constraints and limits? What would we do differently if we were literally starting again?

Once we have pushed our thinking to that extent, we can then land on a creative and **transformaginative** program of work that will deliver **real** innovation. We might even be able to re-use some of that existing structure!

Perfection – a wonderful aspiration

We have spoken about **brilliance** and **excellence** in other parts of this book but I have deliberately avoided talking about **perfection**.

As the heading suggests, perfection is a wonderful aspiration but, sadly, one that is unachievable. We can strive towards it as much as we possibly can – and we should – but, in reality, perfection will always be out of reach.

If that is true, why should we bother aspiring to it?

Because by **aspiring** to perfection and **striving** for perfection, you will engender a continuous improvement mindset for you and for your team.

Acknowledging that perfection **is** unachievable will also give you permission to make a change, a transformation … dare I say, **Transformagination**® … without waiting for all the t's to be crossed and the i's to be dotted.

By definition, **Transformagination**® involves risk. You can't afford to wait for perfection.

Keeping it real

So what are you thinking at this point?

This guy is onto something or **he is living in a fantasy land if he thinks this will work in our organisation**?

Yes, I get it. There **are** real-world constraints in every business. We can't just throw everything out and start again.

But I don't think I have suggested throwing everything out and starting again at any stage of the book. What I have been saying is that if we think **transformaginatively**, you are far more likely to be able to push the boundaries and achieve real transformation in how you operate.

Transformagination® is a mindset. A new way of thinking. A way to strategise that focuses on what we COULD achieve rather than what we SHOULD.

So let's be clear before we move onto the next section. We need to keep it real but there are two ways to approach the solution to any organisational shortcomings:

(1) by starting where we are and thinking about the future from our current vantage point; or

(2) by starting with an ideal, a 'what we could do' perspective and work back from there.

The first of these options is very much the safe way. The existing way. The way that 99.9% of organisations would approach transformation and change.

But we're not like the others. We are **transformaginative** thinkers. We love pushing the boundaries. Being innovative. Being bold. Being inquisitive. Being creative. Being disruptive.

That's where the magic happens.

I acknowledge that practicalities and constraints exist and they may stop us reaching the ultimate, the place we'd really love to be.

But that doesn't stop us from thinking about it.

Imagining it.

Chapter 5

The A to Z of Transformagination®

In this section, I am going to work through the alphabet and discuss one or more words that start with each letter.

While most of the words relate to **Transformagination®**, there'll be a few that are less about **Transformagination®** and more about how I believe business leaders should think.

When deciding whether you are being **transformaginative**, check yourself against these words and discussion points.

A: Adventurous and Apostrophe

Adventurous

One of the hallmarks of going on an adventure is not being

100% certain of where you'll end up or the route you'll take to get there. There'll be times when you feel that you have made a wrong turn or a bad decision. In fact, I suspect there'll be times that you just wish you'd never set out on the adventure.

It's a bit the same with **Transformagination®**. You might have a vague idea of where you want to go and how you want to get there but, until you get started, there is no certainty.

If you are not adventurous in the context of a **Transformagination®** project, you'll probably only end up with a change.

Apostrophe

I spoke about this in an earlier section but it belongs here as well.

While there are some exceptions to this rule, apostrophes overwhelmingly occur in negative words – can't, won't, don't, shouldn't, couldn't, doesn't – or, in some instances, words of regret – should've, could've, would've, might've, didn't.

I think by now you will have noticed that I don't like negative words very much. Rather than can't, won't, don't, shouldn't, couldn't, didn't, I would much rather hear of people telling us what they can, will, do, should, could and did.

As well it saddens me when I hear about individuals or organisations telling me what they could've, should've, might've or would've done.

There will be times where an apostrophe in a word is important but, in our experience, any time that you are using those words, you are limiting your thinking and, as a consequence, your ability to **transformaginate**.

Don't let a pile of apostrophes get in the way of true transformation in your business.

B: Brave and Brilliant

Brave

Closely related to adventurous, being brave is a critical aspect of completing a **Transformagination**®.

The concept of **Transformagination**® requires people to not just step out of their comfort zone but, indeed, to take a flying leap out of it.

As we discussed earlier, **Transformagination**® requires us to let go of the pool's edge, to remove the safety net, to ignore the constraints in our thinking.

We can only do that when we are brave. How brave are you? How brave is your organisation?

Brilliant

There is a section later in this book that talks more about brilliance so I won't labour the point here. Suffice to say that brilliance is a critical component of a successful **Transformagination**®.

I am not necessarily talking about the definition of brilliance that is related to being clever, although that does certainly help.

I am talking about brilliance as in radiance.
The **Transformagination**® process will give people opportunities to shine. To show the way. To lead with intent. That's what I mean by brilliance.

C: Challenge, Creativity and Could

Challenge

The whole discussion around transformation – and certainly **Transformagination**® – should be one centred around challenge.

The easy thing to do when considering a different way of doing something is to minimise how hard you want to push the boundaries. Resistance is inevitable, particularly when you start to really challenge the current state of play, often resulting in smaller, less impactful changes being made.

If we are serious – and I mean, really serious – about **Transformagination**®, you must be ready for that resistance, deal with it and then continue to challenge even further.

And if you call yourself a Change Manager, is it time for you to add three extra letters and become a Challenge Manager? Challenge the approach, challenge the corporate inertia, challenge the resistance. Without challenge, I suspect the opportunity to really transform your business will be missed.

Creativity

If you have made it this far into the book, you'll already realise how important creativity is when delivering **Transformagination**®. Anyone can come up with ideas for change – only a creative thinker can deliver **transformaginative** ideas.

Existing methodologies and protocols often stifle creativity by requiring people to think and work in a tried and tested manner. Calling in an industry expert or a highly credentialed leader to lead a program of work is often done to utilise their knowledge and experience of previous projects, rather than to tap into their creativity to deliver a totally new approach.

Too often I have seen organisations stifling creative ideas in the name of risk management. Now is the time to change that – now is the time to foster and encourage creativity within your organisation.

Could

In a previous section of this book, I spoke about the critical difference between **could** and **should**.

If you find yourself asking what we **should** do or how we **should** be operating our business, there's a fair chance that your business is destined to deliver change. **Should** implies that there is some kind of standard or expectation around how you operate your business.

Changing the word to **could** immediately opens up an opportunity for people to think beyond those standards and expectations.

And that's where the magic lives!

D: Determination, Deliberate and Disruption

Determination

Closely related to brave, determination is another critical trait in taking a **transformaginative** approach to change and transformation.

Brave is about the decision-making process and the preparedness to make a start on doing something truly innovative. Determined is more about an ability to maintain an energy and a focus that enables an organisation to stay on task, to finish the work and deliver the outcome. Bravery without determination makes decisions but does not deliver outcomes. Determination without bravery is often unnecessary.

As many readers would attest, delivering change within an organisation is a tough ask, often met with direct and deliberate resistance. Trying to overcome what I describe as corporate inertia – that need to drive hard to get the ball rolling – requires determination.

Acknowledge the requirement for determination and embrace it. As someone once said – if change or transformation was easy, everyone would be doing it.

Deliberate

Earlier in this book, I suggested that transformation is never an accident.

Change can be accidental. Change can be minor. Change can occur with very little momentum. Change can happen without people noticing.

But transformation is different. It needs a champion – sometimes a superhero – to push on when it gets tough. Transformation can create discomfort and uncertainty.

This is amplified further when we talk about **Transformagination**®. It requires all of this and more.

It must be deliberate and intentional. It must push and, in many cases, go beyond the existing boundaries.

I'll say it again. Deliberate and intentional.

Disruption

Wasn't this the buzz word a few years ago? Businesses declared themselves as disruptors because they changed their logo or they deployed chatbots on their web site. That's not a disruption.

Uber changed the way that we access taxi-like services. Bunnings turned the humble hardware store into something totally different. Apple turned a telephone into a computer in your hand.

These are disruptors.

Transformagination® is where the disruption happens.

Imagine being part of the first conversation about Uber. We had been hailing taxis for decades, either as they drove past or by ringing a telephone operator.

I imagine that the Uber conversation started with 'what would we do differently if we started again'. What if we were able to have anyone book a rideshare with other drivers from their mobile device?

That's not a conversation about changing the phone number to a 13 number. That's not a conversation that says, 'how can we improve taxis'. It threw away the constraints and the people **transformaginated**.

That's true disruption.

E: Excellence and Education

Excellence

Where does the balance between cost and excellence sit within your organisation? I believe that in many instances, they are considered to be mutually exclusive – you can either have excellence or you can have reduced costs.

I disagree with that contention – you **can** have both.

Using the resources you have to produce the very best products and services you are capable of is the pathway to excellence.

There are restaurants that start their wine list at $100 per bottle. There are cars you can buy that, for some people, cost the same as buying a house. There are clothes you can buy that cost what many see as unaffordable. These items are all likely to be excellent.

But at the same time, there are a great number of products and services that are excellent that don't cost anywhere near as much.

Undoubtedly, they are less **exclusive** but are they any less **excellent**?

Excellence is about creating the very best service or product you can, using the resources you have available to you. Exclusivity is about creating something that very few can afford or access.

Every organisation and every individual can strive for excellence in everything they do. This doesn't require anything more than a culture that motivates and truly supports people to be the very best they can be.

Never confuse excellence with exclusivity.

Education

As you will have detected from other parts of this book, I believe that organisations that take a less traditional approach to leadership will be the ones that can truly **transformaginate**.

In traditional organisational structures, you stand a far better chance of becoming a leader by waiting for your turn to come along. You become the leader, often, because you are the most experienced subject matter expert in your department or work stream. You know which levers to pull when things go bad. You know how to deal with most crises because you've seen them all before.

But if we keep on promoting people into leadership

positions based on what has happened in the past, why is it surprising that true **Transformagination®** is hard to do?

Is it time to start being creative not just in ideas but in selecting leaders? And if it is, what are you going to do to make sure that everyone is on board?

Education will play an enormous role in changing that culture. As we have spoken about directly and indirectly elsewhere in this book, if you keep on doing what you've always done, you'll keep on getting what you always got.

The people who are those subject matter experts will continue to be critical to your success. We still need to utilise those skills and that experience and knowledge. But they will also need to be educated that leadership is not necessarily where they will end up – and that's okay. They'll need to be educated that others with less experience might be better suited to taking the company in a different direction.

Likewise, those people who have had their future view obscured by the person standing in front of them in the Great Leadership Queue will also need to be educated. Educated about how to be a good leader. Educated that their ideas are equally valuable. Educated that going in the same direction as their predecessors will not do anything to

transformaginate their organisation.

But before education, there must be willingness and drive. As the reader of this book, you may well need to be the willing and driven person for your organisation.

F: Frustration and Fun

Frustration

Change and transformation activities often create frustration for those impacted but, sometimes, the members of the team who are delivering these programs can be equally frustrated.

Have you stopped to think about why that frustration occurs?

I think it is often caused by a lack of clarity and transparency by the project team and by the leaders who are sponsoring the change program.

Put yourself in the shoes of the impacted colleagues. By the time they first become aware that things are changing, the leadership and project teams are already well down the path towards delivery. The impacted colleagues don't have any context or background for the upcoming change when that news first arrives in their inbox or at their town hall presentation.

Therefore, as part of the project team, when you first engage with them, you need to make sure that everything is explained clearly and without assumptions that they know what you know. If that messaging is not clear and if there are no opportunities for them to seek further information, there is every chance that there will be resistance, leading to frustration for them (we don't know what's happening) and for you (why are these people resisting the change – it makes perfect sense to me).

This is where engagement becomes so much more important than communication. We have spoken about it so many times already in this book but unless there are genuine opportunities for ongoing interaction between the project team and the impacted colleagues (that is, engagement) and not just one-way messages (how many see communications to be), there will be frustration.

Fun

It's easy enough to say but unless you are having some level of fun when delivering a change or transformation program, you are not doing it right. Sure, some elements of delivering a program that impacts on colleagues is anything but fun but without **any** fun, it is going to become tedious and boring pretty quickly.

This is another reason why I think **Transformagination**® is something to embrace. Rather than just spending time delivering a program (just like every other program, using the same tried and tested – or is that tired and tested – methodology), taking some time out to play **what if**, imagining what **could** happen instead of what **should** happen can give people an opportunity to get their creative juices flowing.

And from where I sit, this brings an element of fun to something that can otherwise be pretty hard work.

G: Growth and Greatness

Growth

Think about the organisation you are working for. Do they have a growth mindset?

As I sit here writing, I think about some of the organisations I have worked with over the years and the change and transformation programs I have been involved in. The driving force for so many of those projects was reducing costs and creating efficiencies.

While both of these motivators are worthwhile and, in some cases, business-critical, it seems that there is always some degree of what I called the 'cutback mentality' at play.

Cutback mentality is the polar opposite of a growth mindset. A cutback mentality says, 'what can we get rid of' where a growth mindset says, 'how can we do more'.

Sure, it is important to remove unnecessary costs from your business. Yes, it is important to create efficiencies where it makes sense.

But if you do that without any thought about growing your business, you will eventually get to a point where there is nothing left to cut.

By thinking **transformaginatively**, you are, by definition, displaying a growth mindset. What **could** we do? If we were starting from scratch, how would we set ourselves up?

A growth mindset is a choice. Choose growth over cutback every time.

Greatness

What happened to the aspiration for greatness?

It seems that many organisations operate to catch up with

their competitors rather than taking the plunge and shooting for the stars. I once worked for a company that strove to be number 2 in the market. The reason given was that number 1 can take on the risk of new ideas and if they worked, we could adapt and sit in behind them.

It seems that many organisations are happy in cruise control, tapping the brakes every now and again to avoid disaster. Not getting ahead of themselves and, disappointingly, in many cases, not getting ahead of their competitors.

Transformagination® is based on striving for the absolute best an organisation can be. If we were starting again without any of the legacies, constraints or anything else holding us back, surely, we could aim for greatness.

Think about the vision statement for your organisation. Does it talk about greatness? Having scoured the internet, I have been able to ascertain that many of the big organisations talk about fulfilling potential, being customer-centric, saving the planet and a range of other similar statements.

In the 25 vision statements I found, not one of them used the word 'great' or 'greatness'.

I think everyone should strive for greatness. Sure, not everyone will achieve greatness, nor will everyone agree on the measures that define greatness.

But you know what **you** think greatness looks like. What steps are you taking towards your concept of greatness?

H: Heritage and Hesitation

Heritage

Heritage is an interesting concept and one that often gets in the road of **Transformagination**®. I worked for an organisation a few years ago that had a range of brands in the market, both here in Australia and overseas.

One particular brand was completely off limits when it came to discussing change or transformation (so you can imagine how well **Transformagination**® would have gone in that context). It was one of the oldest brands in the company's portfolio and was allowed to run as it always had. It was costing significantly more to run than any other part of the business but everyone accepted that and worked around it.

Everything we tried to do resulted in the hand brake being gently applied when we got too close to that specific brand. Sometimes, the application of the hand brake was not so gentle.

What happens when heritage and **Transformagination**® come together?

I don't see it as a major issue to be honest. **Transformagination**® says 'let's park all constraints, restrictions and limits while we think'. Yes, we understand that there are realities that will come into play when we finally settle on a strategy for the way forward but while we are thinking, while we are seriously considering what we **could** be doing, even the untouchables need to be set aside for the time being.

Once we have a vision for what we **could** be, we can start to overlay those constraints and see how they impact on our **could be** state.

Hesitation

Hesitation is often a symptom of risk aversion. We get to a point where we need to take a risk and just before we pull the trigger, hesitation kicks in and an opportunity is lost.

Again, there are practicalities, constraints and other limitations that need to be considered before we take the plunge on a change, a transformation and most certainly, a **Transformagination**®. But unnecessary hesitation means that you open the door to your competitors jumping first, your leadership getting cold feet or some other delay being identified.

This is not about recklessly lunging forward without doing an appropriate risk assessment. But let's emphasise the word 'appropriate' in the previous sentence.

Is it appropriate to launch a change or transformation and then fix whatever goes wrong after the event? What is the worst thing that could happen if we launched and it all went wrong?

These are the sorts of questions that you should ask yourself and if the answers are 'yes' and 'nothing terrible', I say 'get this thing done'.

I: Imagination, Innovation and Inertia

Imagination

We have spoken a lot about the importance of imagination in making significant changes to an organisation – indeed, without imagination, **Transformagination**® doesn't exist.

Many organisations say that they encourage and, in some instances, reward imagination but – do they really? If someone truly uses their imagination, are they more likely to be rewarded or ridiculed?

Imagination is not leveraging ideas from another part of the business. Imagination is not copying what your competitors are doing.

Imagination is all about playing a game of 'what if'. Pushing the boundaries. Thinking outside of the box – no, in fact, destroying the box so that there are no constraints.

The great philosopher and more–than–handy scientist, Albert Einstein said it brilliantly – **imagination is more important than knowledge**.

Knowledge refers to a collection of things that people already know, that already exist. Imagination is about inventing ideas from nothing, bringing together components to create something that is bigger and more effective than the individual parts.

Kids imagine all the time. They make up games. They invent imaginary playmates. They can lose themselves in a fantasy world for hours.

When did you last imagine? When did you last set aside time to embrace imagination for yourself and/or for your team? What changed to stop it?

Innovation

Innovation is a concept that has been so watered down in the past twenty years or more that it is virtually unrecognisable. In the same way that 'significant change' has become 'transformation', it seems that innovation has become another word for doing things differently.

In my eyes, innovation cannot occur without imagination. Innovation can only occur on the back of original and creative thinking.

What steps are you taking towards innovation?

Are you allowing people time and space to think creatively? And if you are, are you paying enough attention to the quiet voices – the people who haven't been given the opportunity to be heard before?

Now is the time to start. Embrace creative and unconventional thinking. Embrace true innovation.

Inertia

Inertia is defined as 'a tendency to do nothing or remain unchanged'. In the world of Newtonian physics, it relates to a tendency for an object to continue to be at rest or to continue in the same direction, at the same speed, unless acted upon by an unbalanced force.

I often use the term 'organisational inertia' to describe the difficulty a business has in transforming itself due to the tendency for things to stay as they are. We have all worked for businesses where it's just so much easier to do today what we did yesterday and will do tomorrow, than it is to transform.

Transformation is hard, really hard – if it was easy, everyone would be doing it. But nowhere in that statement have I suggested that it is impossible. We can take some inspiration from Newton that says that an external force will cause an object to change speed or direction.

So, taking the half-full approach … what is the external force you need in your organisation right now? Maybe it is you taking the lead and introducing some truly innovative, truly creative – dare I say – truly **transformaginative** thinking.

One thing we can be certain of … if nothing changes, if no unbalanced force is applied, everything will be the same tomorrow, next week and next month.

Be that unbalanced force!

J: Jump

Jump

There is a well-worn statement that suggests that you should always look to step outside of your comfort zone. I disagree. Stepping outside of your comfort zone only requires a slight adjustment to find yourself back inside it.

I encourage you to take this opportunity to jump out of your comfort zone.

Take a flying leap.

If you jump out of your comfort zone, it is almost certainly non-reversible. It is like leaping from the 10m diving board or skydiving … the jump takes serious commitment but once you've done it, there's no turning back.

I spoke with someone recently who suggested that the best approach when confronted with a challenge is to 'bite off more than you can chew – and then chew like crazy'.

How much are you biting off?

Real transformation – dare I say, **Transformagination**® – requires so much more than nibbling around the edges.

Jumping out of your comfort zone takes a fair bit of courage but if you are not prepared to do that today, when will it be a better time?

K: Kinetic

Kinetic

For those of us who studied secondary school physics, we'd all recognise kinetic as being the form of energy relating to movement, calculated as being ½ multiplied by the mass multiplied by the speed squared.

The word kinetic comes from the Ancient Greek *kinetikos* meaning 'puts in motion'. So much of what we have talked about in this book has been related to getting things moving.

Start the process of **Transformagination**®. Encourage creative and innovative thinking. Be adventurous and brave. Get things in motion.

As we mentioned a couple of sections back, many businesses are held back by an organisational inertia that requires a significant effort – an unbalanced force, to use Newton's term – to get things moving.

What steps are you taking to create some kinetic activity within your organisation? If you don't do it, who will? If now isn't the right time, when will that be?

L: Leadership, Learning and Listen

Leadership

We have spoken about leadership in previous sections of this book so I won't labour the point here.

That said, we need to continue to be mindful that there is a major difference between management and leadership. As we said earlier, we manage things and we lead people.

If you are focusing on **managing** change, then my guess is that you are spending lots of time and effort on creating artefacts like change plans, 'comms' plans, 'BIAs', ensuring that when the project leader or accountable executive asks for an update, you can show them a document that looks impressive and suggests that everything is under control.

If you are focusing on **leading** change, you'll be spending time with impacted people, understanding how the upcoming changes will affect them, working with them to address any resistance, ensuring that they are on-board and supporting you.

When it comes to people, leadership will beat management every single time.

Learning

There's that old cliché that says that you can't teach an old dog new tricks. Not being an expert in canine behaviour, I am ill-equipped to comment on the truth of that statement.

What I can tell you is that there is always scope for people to learn regardless of their age or circumstances. Indeed, when you decide that you have learned enough, I think it's time to hang up the boots and do something else.

In the context of **Transformagination**®, people will need to learn new things. They will need to learn to let go of the past, the heritage, the legacies, the constraints that are inevitable contributors to the corporate inertia I have spoken about. They will need to learn to involve colleagues that weren't necessarily part of previous strategic conversations. They will need to learn that using the word SHOULD is generally very restrictive.

Understand that for some colleagues, particularly those with plenty of experience, all of this may feel a little counterintuitive and challenging. Acknowledge that and work with them to help them learn.

Listen

Listening is a really important part of engagement. As I have said on numerous occasions throughout the book, engagement is far more important than communication in the context of change and transformation projects.

Engagement is two-way. This implies that while you might have important messaging to impart to impacted colleagues, you also have a responsibility to listen.

Listen for feedback about the proposed change. Feedback is not necessarily resistance – it should be considered an opportunity to sense-check your messaging and how these colleagues are feeling about the change.

Listen for questions about the proposed change. This might imply that your messaging is not clear or detailed enough for all colleagues. Again, don't be offended just because there are questions from those impacted. Ensure that you listen and provide answers to the questions you are presented with.

Listen for suggestions that may not have been thought about by the project team. Project teams are often (not always) short on subject matter expertise and they rely on those impacted colleagues for extra knowledge and context.

There is an old saying that says you have one mouth and two ears for a reason. Maybe listening twice as much as speaking is a good place to start.

Another thing that has happened in many projects I have been involved with is that the members of the business leadership team make the strategic decisions and then impose (deliberate choice of word) them via a change or transformation program. Occasionally, other less senior colleagues are invited to scoping sessions or other workshops – but are they listened to? Do they feel comfortable to speak up when other senior colleagues are sitting with them? If they do speak up, are you and your project colleagues listening?

This is, once again, where engagement beats communication every single time. If you are truly **engaging** with these colleagues, they are going to be much more likely to provide the feedback, questions and suggestions. Their feedback, questions and suggestions are often more creative and uninhibited by constraints and legacy activity.

Listen to these colleagues – they might just have a perspective that has not been captured yet.

M: Mediocrity

Mediocrity

Let's start with a reasonably confronting question – **why do so many businesses and individuals accept mediocrity?**

Now, that might be an unfair assessment of your organisation but work with me on this one.

Earlier in this book, I asked how 'fit for purpose' your operating model was – a score out of 100 with no multiples of 5. Did you give your business a score?

If it was better than, let's say 80, it could be said that your organisation only requires some tweaking to move towards 100. That's something to celebrate and to continue to build on.

If it was anything less than 80, it tells me that your business is motoring along, accepting the fact that things could be better – but not doing anything about it.

Mediocrity is all about accepting things for what they are, average, ordinary. Many mediocre businesses achieve acceptable results and feel like that's enough. If that's what you want for your business, that is your decision.

But if you are looking to be better than average, better than ordinary, you need to act. **Now.** Improve your 'fit for purpose' score.

But to do that, you'll need to transform. Do things differently. Innovate. Be creative.

Please don't accept mediocrity. You're better than that.

N: Normal, Now and No

Normal

Remember back when COVID-19 hit, there was a determination – for some, an obsession – to get back to 'normal'.

As we all moved forward to a post-COVID life, it was an amazing opportunity to define a 'new normal' – something that matched or exceeded the expectations of your colleagues, your customers and other individuals and organisations you interact with.

At that time, did you just drift along and accept that whatever happened to your business would become that new normal or did you take decisive action to establish a business model that would work for you and those you serve, going forward?

If you have just drifted into a new normal, I really hope you take some time to read the other part of this section – because I would suggest that there is only one time to stop and take a look at the way your business operates. NOW.

Now

The old cliché 'there's no time like the present' could not be any more applicable.

The past is the past and, while there is plenty to learn from what has happened before, there is nothing we can do to change it.

When it comes to considering the future, I am always reminded of a sign I saw outside a pub in Queensland that said, 'free beer tomorrow'. When I came back the next day, the offer still stood – free beer tomorrow. If we wait until tomorrow to make changes, things will be exactly as they are today, tomorrow.

There is only one time that matters – **now**. Start the process of transformation now and tomorrow, you will have started the journey. As the old Chinese proverb says, 'a journey of a thousand miles starts with a single step'.

Take that step now. Not next week. Not in an hour or two. **NOW**. It is never too early to take the first step.

No

Here is a word that, too often, gets used to stifle change and transformation.

Think back over some of mankind's greatest achievements.

What if Armstrong had said he wanted to stay on Earth?

What if Michelangelo said that he thought that the ceiling of the Sistine Chapel looked okay the way it already was.

What if some of the great explorers had stayed at home?

Too often people say 'no' to stop things changing or because they can't be bothered. At other times people say 'no' because it is too hard to say 'yes'.

I like to think that the default position for most change and transformation leaders is 'yes' not 'no'. I absolutely know that **transformaginative** thinkers always say 'yes' by default!

Where do you sit on that one?

O: Organisation and Opportunity

Organisation

Typically, in the corporate world, organisations are presented as a hierarchy, the so-called 'org chart' is made up of a series of boxes with names and titles written in them – the more senior the person, the closer to the top of the diagram they will be.

Consider the attributes that key corporate influencers have enjoyed over the years. They were typically close to the top of that org chart, they were typically older, more often than not male and they possessed years of experience, either within the organisation or the same industry sector. They knew how to make decisions that would maintain the status quo or, at best, to make changes with an eye on what they knew would work.

But think now of this through the lens of **Transformagination®**.

I am comfortable that the org chart remains an important document from an **accountability** perspective. But from an **influence** perspective, I'd like to see the value of the org chart played down.

If we are being **truly transformaginative**, the value of NOT being constrained by history, experience, heritage, etc.

will be equally important. No one is denying the value of experience and this, along with accountability, is typically reflected in a colleague's salary. That said, I'd contend going forward, NOT knowing what used to work is also going to be invaluable to all organisations.

People who haven't been sitting at the top of the org chart are often going to have different ideas. Often really innovative ideas. They won't be constrained by what they **should** be doing.

Rather than relying on the tried and tested, the individuals and teams who can deliver true innovation, true transformation – they are going to be the influencers.

And that might come from the bottom of the chart, not the top.

I'll have more to say about org charts and the shape of roles in Chapter 6.

Opportunity

What a great word.

As I have said elsewhere, you shouldn't wait for opportunity to knock on your door, as the idiom suggests it might. You should always have that door open, with one eye trained on the door at all times.

Given the speed at which life travels, it is likely that, if an opportunity arises, it isn't going to be there for long. Grab it, run with it and make every post a winner because, in my mind, there are not too many things that are sadder than a missed opportunity.

P: Processes, Procedures and Protocols

These three factors are so closely linked in the world of change, transformation and **Transformagination**®, that we may as well consider them simultaneously.

These three concepts are, individually and collectively, amongst the biggest speed humps in delivering change.

I have spoken at length about how I prefer the word **could** over the word **should**. **Could** talks about the open-ended. Nothing is off the table when we are considering **could**.

In contrast, **should** implies that there are rules or expectations that must be adhered to as we consider the way forward. Often these rules and expectations are rooted in the processes, procedures and protocols that are in place within organisations.

How often do you hear 'that's not how we do things' or 'you

must fill out this form to move forward', etc.

I am not advocating that you should throw out existing processes, procedures or protocols, especially those that exist to ensure safety or adherence to regulations and laws. Instead, I am encouraging you to seriously question every single one of them to ensure that they are there for the right reason and not to tie the business down to 'the old way'.

Q: Question

Question

As we move forward with a **transformaginative** mindset, there is a well-worn question that needs to be superseded. That question is … Why?

Why can be used as an investigative tool but more often than not, it becomes a roadblock. When an innovative idea is tabled, if enough people ask **why**, it will eventually create sufficient doubt in the minds of risk-averse leaders to block the idea from proceeding.

But to borrow from President John F Kennedy, rather than asking **why**, it might be time to respond to innovative ideas with **why not**.

Rather than trying to dredge up reasons to block a radical and creative idea, a **transformaginative** mindset will move to a default position of 'Let's give this a go. Why not?'

Imagine what could go **right** if we worked with a default position of **why not**. That's an environment where **Transformagination**® has a real opportunity to flourish.

R: Resistance, Resolve and Radical

Back when I was a boy, we had the three Rs at school – reading, writing and arithmetic. Ironically, given that these were supposed to be the bedrock of all education, only one the three actually starts with the letter R!

That aside, let's consider three other Rs that belong in this book.

Resistance

Resistance is inevitable whenever true transformation is on the agenda. Everyone loves the security of what they know and trust but when the change manager, transformation lead or **transformaginist** steps up, resistance will very likely be a prominent feature of meetings and other conversations.

There are two ways this could go and it will be up to each impacted colleague to make their individual choice.

One option is for them to try even harder to hold onto any small remaining piece of their security blanket which will inevitably lead to even higher levels of resistance. Others will choose to take an opportunity to acknowledge that their safety net has been torn away and will at least try hard to embrace the changes that are inevitable.

Where do you sit on this one? It really is a choice you can make.

Resolve

Closely linked to other words like determination and bravery, resolve is a hallmark of successful transformation programs. Resolve is defined as a firm determination to do something. Without it, businesses will drift along and never really settle on a way forward.

Identify the colleagues who display resolve and, just as a tip, don't always look at the top of the organisation. There are people with resolve throughout your organisation. Find them and engage them in your transformation program.

Radical

Radical is often seen as the polar opposite of conservative and therefore seen by many as being a bad thing. Certainly people of my parents' vintage saw radicalism as what was going to bring society, as we knew it, to its knees.

If we are serious about **Transformagination**®, we absolutely need to behave in a manner that is the polar opposite of conservative.

Conventional thinking is the first cousin of conservative behaviour. We need to think radically (or unconventionally if you prefer) if we want our business to stand out from the crowd. Many organisations have developed their point of difference based on what used to be – history, reliability, experience.

That is not going to work anymore. It's time to think radically. What could you be doing to make your business great?

S: Should and Stride

Should

As you have no doubt read, **should** is a word that really

frustrates me.

Should implies an adherence to some rules or expectations – we should do this (why?), we shouldn't do that (why not?).

In contrast, **could** is open ended. **Could** allows people to be creative and innovative. **Could** requires imagination.

Next time you are tempted to use the word **should**, take a moment to consider whether **could** is a better option. Change the way you think – don't look back for validation, look forward for possibilities.

Stride

And when you are looking at future strategies, don't dawdle towards a strategy that keeps one hand holding onto the side of the pool.

Take strides. Big strides.

T: Transformagination®

Transformagination®

Well, here it is. The big one. The bringing together of two critical concepts to create one – transformation and imagination. Transformation without imagination is just that – a change that makes something completely different but always with one eye on the past and the constraints that accompany that approach.

Transformation with imagination – **Transformagination®** – is not constrained. It is transformation without limits. Nothing is impossible in a world based on **Transformagination®**.

It's a massive mindset change but one I think you'll find motivating, exciting and challenging all at once.

U: Untypical and Uncomfortable

Untypical

I liked the word so much, I named my company **Untypical**. Yes, it is the opposite of typical and a synonym of the more common **atypical** but I thought that it would make more sense to use the less common antonym. The untypical atypical, if you will.

Typical implies doing something the way everyone else does. Typical means a common approach. Typical and **Transformagination®** don't belong together.

On the other hand, untypical is everything that **Transformagination**® sets out to achieve. My company is proud to be Untypical by name and, more importantly, untypical by nature.

Uncomfortable

Now that you have got this far into the book, I really, really hope that some of what I have said has made you feel uncomfortable.

You can have comfortable change. It is difficult to have comfortable transformation. It is impossible to have comfortable **Transformagination**®.

If you are working on a program of work in which you feel comfortable, I would strongly suggest that you are working on a change program. That's fine, as long as you realise that what you are doing is NOT a transformation.

I am a great believer in the idiom that, if transformation was easy (read, comfortable), then everyone would be doing it.

You will only achieve transformation and, indeed, **Transformagination**® by getting uncomfortable. Embrace the discomfort. Do great things.

V: Visionary and Versatile

Visionary

I think you know where I am going with this one.

No one can be **transformaginative** without being a visionary.

Visionary is a word that gets overused and dramatically overplayed. In the same way as transformation has been hijacked by minor change programs, visionary seems to be used to describe anyone with a good idea.

But surely, visionary is something quite different. Something so much more that having a good idea.

I think that a visionary is someone who sees things that other people don't. Things that are truly innovative. And let's call it out, things that are often risky.

But without risk, there can be no true transformation. In every organisation, there will be visionary thinkers who continue to be ignored or are too afraid to even raise their truly innovative ideas for fear of ridicule or rejection.

Find those visionary thinkers in your organisation. Embrace their ideas. Be pushed well beyond your comfort zone.

Seriously consider what they are saying because they might just have an idea that enables you to truly transform your business in a way that you never even imagined.

Versatile

This is such an undervalued attribute when companies are recruiting for a change or transformation team. Yes, I understand that having experience and, to a lesser extent, formal qualifications in change are important but so is versatility.

Change Leaders are often the ones who are required to provide the glue between the building blocks. They often need to be able to do lots of different things that other colleagues don't see as being within their job description.

If you recruit a change leader who can only operate in their own change-focused swim lane, you are probably doing yourself and your project/project team a significant disservice.

Look for people who can lead change but who have a wide range of experiences in different roles, different industries and different organisations. They will be the ones who are often the best equipped to drive transformation in your organisation.

W: Wisdom and Willingness

Wisdom

Who provides the wisdom within your business?

I think that there are many organisations that feel that unless the wisdom is coming from the top of the organisation, it can't really be considered wisdom.

But there is wisdom throughout the organisation. People who have come from other organisations. People who have thought creatively and innovatively. People who have probably wanted to say things in the past but haven't had the opportunity.

Seek out the wisdom of those people. Encourage them to make suggestions. Give them space and permission to bring their ideas to the table.

Now, you might be thinking 'we've always given our people the chance to give us suggestions, submit ideas and provide feedback'.

Yes, but have you?

Imagine you are a younger person lost in the middle-to-lower layers of the organisational diagram, are you going to speak up? Are you really going to feel comfortable questioning existing processes and policies? If you are in a workshop or other environment where you are surrounded by executives and other senior leaders, are you going to feel comfortable contributing to the conversations?

Will these colleagues really be given an opportunity to contribute?

Maybe they will. More likely they won't. And if they won't, that is a pile of wisdom you've missed out on.

Willingness

Everything that I have spoken about in this book requires a high degree of willingness to accept that transformation is necessary for so many businesses. As a result, an equal level of willingness is required from the people within those businesses, to work together towards that transformed business model.

As I mentioned elsewhere, there is an inertial state that many organisations find themselves in – a state where it is just too hard to take the steps towards transformation. To overcome that inertia, everyone needs to be clearly focused on the same direction and the same outcomes.

That doesn't mean that the CEO or senior management

team needs to make a decree and assume that everyone will fall into line. It means working with people across the organisation to develop a shared vision and then encouraging a willingness by everyone to embrace it.

Without that level of willingness, there will be a huge amount of energy expended and very little will change.

What are you doing within your organisation to ensure that willingness?

X: Xenacious

Xenacious

You thought that I'd struggle to come up with an X word, didn't you? My friend and customer service guru, Cate Schreck, used the word **X-factor** in her very excellent book **The A to Z of Service Excellence** so I had to look for something else. Xylophone wasn't an option and so I went looking and found **xenacious**.

Xenacious is defined by Merriam-Webster's Word Central site as 'filled with a yearning for change'. How xenacious are you? How xenacious is your organisation?

If you are not filled with a **yearning** for change, I think you are going to find it difficult to make change, let alone transformation.

I think that it is the most xenacious organisations who will be able to deliver exceptional change and transformation. They are organisations that don't just do change because it is forced upon them. They are organisations that embrace and really look for transformation opportunities.

Be xenacious!

Y: Young and Yes

Young

For as long as I can remember, the people who made the decisions and set the direction for a business, especially in the bigger corporates, were those with the greatest experience, either within the organisation or the relevant industry sector. Most often, this has been allowed to happen because they can look at a scenario and, using their experience of similar circumstances, determine the right way forward.

With respect, is that tried-and-true (tired-and-true, maybe?) experience as valuable as it once was? Much of it was based on a strong knowledge of processes, procedures, policies and protocols that used to work.

If we are serious about transformation and, dare I suggest, **Transformagination**®, I think we need to loosen our grip on existing knowledge of processes, procedures, policies and protocols.

Now is as good a time as any to consider the input of some of your younger colleagues … people whose thinking has not been framed by those existing practices. People who have fresh ideas. People whose experience is limited but whose energy levels are typically high.

Are there some younger colleagues in your team who could add real value to your **transformaginative** planning?

Yes

Our other Y word is one that doesn't get used anywhere near as often as I think it should.

Yes. In most organisations, where new and creative ideas are floated, the default position is No.

If you are serious about transformation, now is the time to turn that around. Take some risks. **Say yes**.

We've already talked about being brave and creative in

previous sections of this book. Now is the time to start saying **yes** to innovation.

Z: Zealous and Zoom

Zealous

As I suggested elsewhere, transformation doesn't happen by accident. It requires a deliberate effort to change things dramatically.

The other thing that transformation requires is zeal – a word we don't use very often anymore. In fact, a zealot – a person who displays zeal – is often a term of ridicule for a person who borders on a fanatical desire to achieve something.

But zeal is what is required for true transformation.

Remember, that there will always be active resistance to transformation. There'll also be passive or inertial resistance to transformation. But as I hope you'll agree by now, without transformation – I think, **Transformagination**® – your organisation will drift along, showing a tendency to stay exactly where you are.

And is that what you want? Is that what your business requires? I think not.

So, become a zealot. Become fanatical about the transformation that your organisation requires. Ignore the ridicule. Fight against the inevitable inertia and resistance that you'll encounter.

Or pretty much keep drifting.

Zoom

It is the name of a product that has become a critical part of most organisations' communication strategies during the past decade, enabling people to meet virtually and work from just about anywhere. But that's not the Zoom I'm talking about here.

I'm talking about the zoom that comes by pressing the accelerator. There are many organisations who are, to use the motoring analogy, allowing their engines to idle. There are others who haven't yet moved beyond second gear.

The organisations who can set their direction and press that accelerator are the ones that are going to leave their competitors behind. The ones that are going to get to where they need to be, sooner.

Don't drift. Don't idle. It's time to zoom.

Chapter 6

Some Other Thoughts

If you have made it all the way to this stage of the book, I have a few other thoughts to share. Not so much related to change, transformation or, indeed, **Transformagination**®, however, I believe some worthwhile considerations about how you conduct yourself in your day-to-day life in business.

Fitting stars into rectangular boxes

Have you ever noticed how organisational diagrams (or organigrams as some companies like to call them) always use rectangular boxes to represent roles? Have you also noticed that those boxes are placed in such a way as to identify who reports to who?

Well, 1987 has just called and wants its idea back.

If you haven't already worked it out, I am not a big fan of

conventional thinking. Sure conventional thinking has its place – it provides certainty, structure, security and all those other things that worked so much better in the 80s and 90s than they do in the here and now.

But conventional thinking also introduces constraints and rigidity that stops us being truly creative in how we run our business.

Going back to the rectangular nature of the traditional organisational diagram … have you ever heard the old saying about fitting square pegs into round holes?

Well, how about stars into rectangular boxes?

Yes, a significant number of your colleagues will be quite rectangular in the way they work. They will align with the expectations of the rectangular role, doing what the role requires them to do and 'getting the job done'. These people play a critical role in maintaining the stability of a team but **what about the stars**?

What do we know about stars? Some stars have five points, some have more. If you try to fit a star into a rectangular box, they either leave a lot of blank space around them or they stick out of the rectangle – maybe both.

The stars are the people who are going to change the world.

They are the ones that will challenge the status quo. They will be the ones who have the big ideas. They are the ones who will drive transformation. If you are really lucky – and you give them the space – these are the people who can deliver **Transformagination®**.

If you keep constraining stars with boring rectangular roles, I can guarantee that they will either burst out of the rectangle or go and find another organisation – one that values and supports stars.

The other thing about true stars is their capacity to work across all levels of an organisation. They are the ones who are equally comfortable engaging with senior leaders of an organisation as they are with entry level colleagues.

While the requirement for people leadership is important for direction, strategy alignment and professional development, are you creating an environment where stars can shine brilliantly or are they stuck in a structure that stops them from having the impact that they could (not should) have?

It would be like buying a high-powered and luxurious sports car and only ever using it to drive to the local shops and back. You have invested in something (someone) who is capable of so much and yet, you insist on restricting its (their) scope to the mundane.

Maybe it's time for organisations to bite the bullet and specify some roles to be star roles. Identify the stars in your organisation (and outside, too) and let them do their thing, unconstrained by the rectangle and the structure.

Just imagine the level of disruption that could create!

Same recipe = same cake

You get all of the ingredients lined up ready to go. You mix them together like you have so many times before. You pour them into a cake tin and place it in the pre-heated oven for the same length of time as you always do.

And yet, when you open the oven, you seem surprised that, just like last time, you have a magnificent fruit cake. Not a carrot cake or a sponge like Grandma used to make.

Of course you get the same cake – because you used the same recipe!

When you use the same recipe, you get the same cake. If you want something different, you'll need to change the ingredients. If you want a totally different outcome, you'll need a totally different recipe.

Why am I stating the obvious here? It is because I have seen business leaders, project managers, change managers and all sorts of other people continuing to do what they have always been doing and hoping (surely, they can't be **expecting**) that something different will happen.

Same recipe equals same cake. Same business processes, procedures, methodologies, systems and protocols equal the same outcomes.

On Being an Anti-Complexificationist

Okay, so the word complexification may not appear in your dictionary so let me define it for you:

> *COMPLEXIFICATION – the often-subconscious urge to take something that was once simple, re-engineer it and produce a result that is significantly more complex than the original version. It is the direct opposite of simplification (the deliberate act of taking something complex and making it simple).*

Think about your job. Of course, everything seems pretty simple and straightforward to you. You can probably explain

– from your perspective – why a customer needs to speak to five different people to get something done.

But think about your customer for a minute. Suppose they arrived at your office and asked you to explain the process to them, particularly the bit about why they have to bounce from department to department. The only KPIs they care about is how quick and easy it is for them to 'get in and get out' with a result that pleases them.

Maybe there's a belief that consistency of approach can only occur when there is a process in place that is so rigid, so complex and so inflexible that nobody can move without reference to a set of rules and pre-defined documents (now apparently called artefacts). Maybe consulting firms have convinced gullible clients that unless the process is ridiculously complex, it can't possibly be useful. Maybe the complexificationists are starting to take over the business world.

When the complexificationists get their way, processes become more convoluted that they need to be. People can't possibly take in everything about the process so they just learn their little bit and operate in isolation from everyone else.

I worked as a Business Analyst on a project once where my

functional specification document had to be peer reviewed. I'm okay with a peer review but when I turned up at the review meeting to be confronted by 17 colleagues – yes, 17 – I was, to say the least, a little surprised. I was even more surprised when I was told that two sections of my specification were out of sequence. We would have to re-schedule the review because until I had reversed their sequence, we couldn't possibly continue.

I suggested that we could go ahead and review the document, pretending that they were in the correct sequence but was told no – we couldn't do that. We had to follow a process that even had the sequence of document sections defined to that level of complexity, even when the document was still in draft form. You can imagine how easy (not at all) it is to re-schedule 18 people to be in the same room at the same time. I never did find out whether they re-scheduled or not – we agreed that as a devout anti-complexificationist, I was never going to enjoy being part of that program and so I moved onto a new one.

Where do you sit on this? Are you a complexificationist or are you with me on this one? Do you get excited about the opportunity to make things so much more complex than they need to be or are you out there helping me to reduce complexity in business processes and procedures?

If you are ready to join me in the anti-complexification movement, it's time to take positive action and here it is.

Your challenge for this week, should you choose to accept it, is this.

Think of one thing within the scope of your job and identify the unnecessary complexities within the task or activity. GET RID OF THEM. No, that is not a typing error. GET RID OF THE UNNECESSARY COMPLEXITIES (sorry if I am shouting). Take a deep breath and de-complexify whatever you can.

Sure, you might feel like you're letting go of a security blanket or your personal power base. It may provide some discomfort for you. But just think how much happier your clients and customers will be.

And you know what happens when they are happy …

All in all, you're just another brick in the wall**

Why, in business, do we continually use euphemisms for people?

Over the years, I've been an employee, a contractor (both are statements of my contractual arrangements), a human resource (all in all, you're just another brick in the wall), a member of the workforce, part of the headcount, part of the human capital (yes, seriously!), a cost, an overhead, an FTE (for a while, I was only part of an FTE!) … the list goes on and on.

In so many ways, dehumanising the workforce makes life a lot easier. Downsizing the workforce by 20% is so much easier than telling 25 people that you don't need them to work for you anymore. Reducing the headcount is a mathematical and cost reduction activity whereas asking those people to find another job usually involves some emotions, at least for the person who is being asked to leave.

I really believe that people function best when they are treated as a person and not just another resource (like a chair, a PC or a desk).

Sure, treating a colleague as a person instead of a resource means taking their family commitments into account when asking them to work back late. Remembering that a person is really tired because they are coming off a bout of illness requires a human element. As a parent of a year 12 student approaching final exams, your colleague might need some support and encouragement. As part of the headcount or as an overhead, they won't need that consideration.

But, that said, a person has so much more to offer your organisation than a human resource might. Maybe they went through the year 12 thing last year and can empathise with their colleague this year. Maybe someone who has just had a break and is feeling refreshed can take some of the routine stuff from the person who's been under the weather and give them a chance to recover fully.

This is the stuff that only people can do … it is not the stuff that your FTE workforce understands.

And what is with the expression HR Manager? If being a human resource isn't bad enough – what about being an HR?

About 30 years ago, I completed a 'Four Quadrant Leadership' program, conducted by Wilfred Jarvis from Wilfred Jarvis and Associates. One of the key messages I remember from that program was that you manage things but you lead people.

I absolutely agree that if you are responsible for one or more people, you need to manage the costs they incur, the sales targets they aspire to, the budgets you're working within, even in some cases, the workload they need to complete.

But … and this is the big but … managing them as resources can only occur if you de-humanise them and make them some**thing** instead of some**one**.

Another interesting aspect of the 'leadership vs management' question is this – have you ever heard of someone being a micro-leader?

We have all heard how hard it can be when you are being 'micro-managed' – that is, someone looking over your shoulder all the time, making sure that you are on task, controlling how you do things, displaying poor levels of trust, etc. You feel constrained, unable to make your own decisions, unable to manage your own workload – all of which seems to be deeply de-motivating.

So can you be a micro-leader?

No, I don't think it is possible. When you treat colleagues as people rather than resources/FTEs/HRs/etc, it is really hard to micro-lead them. You'll be inclined towards trust, delegation, engagement, involvement and all of those other people-focused traits of a leader, not a manager.

*** With acknowledgement to the great Pink Floyd and, specifically, Roger Waters for the title, taken from his song 'Another Brick In The Wall (Part II)' from the 1979 album, 'The Wall'.*

Different is not wrong

Leading on from being another brick in the wall, is a somewhat related topic – the question of thinking differently.

In many organisations, there seems to be a groupthink approach where everyone thinks the same way, often in deference to what the senior leaders say.

Now, I am not advocating for civil disobedience or mutiny here but if we all think the same way and therefore, do the same thing, we will inevitably end up with the same outcomes. Someone has to think differently if things are going to be different.

If you think differently in your organisation, are you seen to be **different** or **wrong**?

In too many organisations, people who think differently **are** considered wrong. This immediately stifles creative thinking and real innovation.

As a leader, what are **you** doing to encourage your colleagues to share their creative thinking? What steps are **you** taking to not just tolerate people thinking differently but to embrace and celebrate it?

If you don't provide opportunities to let your people think differently and to express their ideas and feedback, they will either stop thinking creatively (the suppression of great ideas) or go somewhere where they are encouraged to do it (the disappearance of great ideas).

Either way, your organisation loses and you stay exactly where you are, doing what you always do.

Brilliant

What a great word – brilliant!

There are two quite distinct meanings (probably more) of the word – one to do with intelligence and ability and the other to do with glittering, sparkling and shining brightly.

If we consider the first meaning, we can't really choose to be brilliant at everything. We have a natural aptitude in some areas, we can train or educate ourselves to be brilliant in others but at the end of the day, we are limited in our capacity to be brilliant in that sense.

But considering the other definition, we **can** choose to be brilliant in everything we do. We can choose our attitude, our approach and, as a direct result, the impact we have on those we live with, work with or socialise with.

How often do you walk into your workplace and see the eyes of your colleagues looking dull and see them just going through the motions? More importantly, how often do your colleagues see the same when they look at you?

Brilliant performance creates brilliant results. Brilliant performance can inspire brilliance in others. Brilliance in a dark place creates light.

This week, choose something that you're going to do and make a conscious effort to do it brilliantly. Look at the impact it has on you and those around you.

And if it doesn't have a positive impact on the outcome, I'll be amazed.

So, who's really important

A client was recently telling me about a conversation he overheard in his workplace which brought back a memory of the first day of my second year of teaching – in February 1985.

Firstly, the recent conversation as told to me by my client:

> *'A new employee was being introduced to some of the people she was going to be working with and after providing the name of each person, the introducer told her that they were the senior, the officer and the assistant. Nothing more was said. No mention of what each of these people did. No mention of how the new employee might interact with each person … just a statement of rank and implied importance.'*

Wow! I can understand how this might be a little more relevant in the military or some other rank-conscious context but, in an office environment, I was really surprised to hear that this was the most significant (only?) piece of information to be given out to the new employee.

In 1985, I was a foundation member of staff in a brand-new secondary school and sitting with me around the table on day 1 was the principal and 15 other people with whom I was going to work to create a new school. The principal started his introduction with a piece of wisdom that I still subscribe to today:

*'There are 17 of us here with different levels
of experience, different levels of knowledge
in our areas of expertise, different levels of
responsibility and, consequently, different scales
of pay. The one thing that is equal amongst us,
though, is our level of importance in achieving
our goal.'*

As a young member of staff, it was a real boost to my
self-esteem to think that, despite my tender years and
minimal experience, I was still just as important as everyone
else.

What is it like in your workplace? Are people valued and
made to feel important despite the position they occupy in
the organisational diagram? Is there an implied importance
attached to the person who sits in the box at the top of the
organisational diagram? Do the folk whose names appear at
the bottom of the organisational chart feel like they are an
important part of the overall team?

A good test is what I call the 'management laugh' test. If a
senior member of staff gets up to present a 'town hall' or
similar, they will invariably start off with a feeble attempt
at humour. Equally invariable is the usual reaction from
everyone around, laughing as though it is the funniest thing

they've ever heard (even though, nine times out of ten, it just isn't funny). Meanwhile, Sally or John from Accounts Payable says something really funny and they are ignored.

Don't get me wrong – I absolutely recognise the senior leader's level of responsibility and accountability and the level of respect they deserve in taking the lead role in an organisation or division.

But ask yourself this question – are they any more **important** than the person who drives the delivery van (that is, the person who has direct interaction with your customers), the cleaner (that is, the person who looks after your health and well–being) or the mail clerk (that is, the person who plays a key role in communication within the office and beyond)?

I think not.

Don't ever confuse accountability and responsibility with importance.

What's your beach ball?

How many emails do you get each day? For most people, the answer is 'far too many'. And, of the emails you get, what proportion are written in the same black font? 80%? 90%?

Of the emails that you receive, what proportion of them do

you read, digest and act upon? 10%? 20%?

It seems to me that email is becoming (has become?) just another form of 'white noise'. Sure, every now and again, you'll see an email from your boss or an important client which will grab your attention. You might even have a rule set up within your email program to highlight those ones. But how much critical information is just getting lost in the flood?

I live quite close to the beach in Geelong and it provides an ideal setting for this illustration.

Suppose I was to wander down to the water's edge with a bottle of drinking water and tip it into the sea. Immediately, that 600ml of water is lost – gone, untraceable and completely ignored. That is very similar to most of the 'white noise' emails that are quickly gone, untraceable and completely ignored, even though they are right there in front of you.

Suppose, instead, I was to head down to the beach with a bottle of raspberry lemonade and tip that into the sea. For a brief moment, a very brief moment, that red liquid would be detectable in the water but a few waves later, it is as detectable as the 600ml of water. This equates to receiving an email with a clever subject or a coloured heading that shows up in the reading pane. It grabs your attention for a moment but then the next wave of emails comes through and it is lost amongst the others.

Instead, if I wander down to the beach and throw a beach ball into the water, it is going to sit there, visible and prominent. It will be the first thing that catches your attention when you look into the sea.

I recently worked on a major transformation program with around 7000 impacted clients, each of whom worked within an independently owned business. They are continually bombarded with emails from our organisation, from their product suppliers and from their customers. Given the importance of engaging these people throughout our program, we needed something that could be our beach ball.

It might be something quite simple – in the end, we found that our beach ball was the use of SMS prompts to our 7000 individuals. We weren't able to get enough information into the SMS message itself but we were able to prompt each person to check their inbox for an email from our program email address. We don't have statistics on the uptake but, anecdotally, the feedback we received was very positive.

Think about your next communications exercise. **What's your beach ball?**

Everybody's working on the weekend

It was Loverboy who, in 1982, had a hit with the song 'Working For The Weekend' but, all these years later, it seems that their sentiment has been replaced for many people. It seems that for many, there is an expectation that 'everybody's working **on** the weekend' … and in many cases, after hours during the week as well.

Why have we allowed this to happen? At a time when businesses are, more than ever, making a stand to support the mental health and wellbeing of their employees, many of my friends and associates are telling me that they go home and get the laptop out so that they can get a couple of hours extra work done after dinner.

At a time when some countries are working towards four-day weeks and six-hour workdays, I see people working many hours beyond what they are paid to do. At a time when obesity is becoming a major health issue, I see people using their leisure time to sit in front of their work computer instead of getting out and doing something active.

Now, I get it when you are running a small business, especially during its period of establishment. The whole 'working in the business vs working on the business' dilemma means that you often find yourself working the extra hours – but that is a choice you make on a project that typically involves your passion and/or your determination to get a new business up and running. But these are not the people I am talking about.

I am talking about mid-range to senior employees in a range of organisations across many different industries, feeling that there is an expectation – typically unstated in employment contracts – that you complete a full day's work in the office and then go home and keep going. That you'll get the laptop or tablet out on Sunday evening, withdraw yourself from family activities and get your email under control for Monday morning.

I put the blame on a couple of factors here.

First of all, many larger organisations run platforms like Microsoft's Viva Engage (and there are others) which are designed to provide a sense of community and a forum for news, thoughts, updates and leader communications.

One of the advantages of this approach is that instead of emails going backwards and forwards, people can share their news and views in a central location. The downside is that some of these platforms seem to insist on telling you every time there is either an 'important update' or when you have chosen not to log in to the platform for a day or two. So, like clockwork, throughout Sunday (because it has been a day or two), the notifications start popping up on people's phones that there are updates – some of them 'important updates' – waiting to be read. Most of them are only considered 'important' because they have been posted by someone on a pre-defined list of executives and other senior leaders.

But I also point the finger at senior leaders themselves. They may choose to get their laptop out on a Saturday afternoon or Sunday night and get themselves a head start on their week. They may choose to log on after hours during the week to keep on top of their workload. But the problem is that this means that their example is often being followed by their colleagues. It almost seems that if Helen or David are sending emails during the evening or weekend, I should be too.

I'm sure that if I mentioned this to Helen or David, they would tell me that they aren't expecting their teams to do that – but that's not the point. Many employees, certainly some of the younger ones who are aspiring to a leadership position, see this as normal behaviour.

One counter argument is that it suits the leader and/or the employee better to work flexibly **and if that is truly the**

case, I am all for it. If someone wants to start their day later so that they can spend time at the gym and catch up on their work later in the day, I'm very happy to hear it. If someone wants to have breakfast with their kids, drop them off at school and then catch up on work after they've gone to bed on Sunday night, absolutely go for it.

My concern is not for people doing work at home or outside of 'normal hours'. My concern is about what appears to be a growing expectation that people are paid to do a full-time job and then they are expected to go above and beyond at the expense of spending time with their family and friends, at the expense of being able to get to the gym or go for a walk, at the expense of being able to participate in a hobby or club.

If this sounds like you, **ask yourself why you are doing it**. Is it because it is expected of you? Is it because you think it is the right thing to do, to show how committed you are to your job? Is it because you have fallen into a bad habit? If you are a leader, have you considered what impact your work habits are having on your teams?

These are questions that, in my mind, are critical indicators of an organisation's culture. It ties in with my earlier thoughts about treating the people who work with you as people and not resources, workforce, FTEs or any of the other euphemisms that are regularly used. Your colleagues are first and foremost people and their work should only represent an appropriate proportion of what they do with their week.

Are you allowing them to do that? Are you allowing **yourself** to do that?

Really busy

In the last section, I called out what I think is a growing trend of people being asked/expected/pressured into working after hours and on their weekends. Whilst it may not be written into their job descriptions, it seems that many, many people are heading home after a day's work and getting their laptop out. Others are firing up their email on Sunday to get a head start for the week.

A related trend, in my mind, is the apparent epidemic of people saying how busy they are. When you get into a lift at work, you might ask a colleague 'how are you?'. More often than not, the response will be 'really busy at the moment'. Now recognising that 'busy' is a relative term – what I call busy may not be what others call busy – how is that the correct response to 'how are you?'?

And while the traditional option – 'Good, thanks. How about you?' – is arguably no more informative of your colleague's wellbeing, why has our response now turned from how we are feeling to how busy we feel we are?

Interestingly, I don't recall anyone ever saying to me that they AREN'T really busy – only that they are. So why has it come to this, I wonder?

Is it because we are trying to impress our colleagues and our friends? Is it because we need to reassure ourselves that we are contributing? Is it that you don't want to tell people how you are really feeling and 'really busy' provides an ideal substitute answer? Is it because how we are seen by those around us is more important than how we feel AND being busy is how you want those around you to see you?

I seriously don't know the answer, but it does concern me a little.

Am I drawing too much of a long bow to suggest that at the same time as 'Really Busy' has become a thing, we have also anecdotally seen an increase in the number of people reporting symptoms of poor mental wellbeing? Is it a coincidence that the RUOK Day has been established at the same time as people are telling their friends and colleagues how busy they are rather than how they are feeling?

As I said above, I don't have the answers to these questions. I simply throw them out there to, hopefully, make you think.

The next time someone asks you how you are, is 'really busy' the correct response or should you take the opportunity to let them know? Next time someone tells you that they are really busy, should you be taking THAT chance to probe a little further, in case being 'really busy' is creating pressure and stress in their lives?

Please take some time to find out how your friends and colleagues are instead of how busy they are. You never know just how important that conversation might be.

Tell me about it (even though I am not really listening)

Closely related to the previous 'really busy' section, is the 'tell me about it' movement.

Colleague: How are you?
You: Really busy.
Colleague: Oh, yeah. Tell me about it.

So, two things fall out of this.

Firstly, 'tell me about it' can often be loosely translated to 'you think you're busy … wait until I tell you how busy I am'.

It seems that being 'really busy' is now a competition. If you say that you are really busy, why should your colleague try and out do you? Is it a contest to see who is busier and, if so, what is the prize? A sense of achievement that you are busier than them? I'm not exactly sure why this is the way many conversations are conducted.

The other puzzling aspect of this response is taking the invitation literally. Next time someone says, 'tell me about it', do it – go ahead and tell them about it. In my experience people who say 'tell me about it' don't actually want you to do anything of the sort. If anything, they want you to STOP telling them about it and start listening to the list of things they have on their plate.

It is a most peculiar response in this context. If I say to someone that I have had a really bad day or that I am really tired, if they say, 'tell me about it', I'm taking that as an invitation not a contest.

Next time someone tells you how they are feeling – even if it is 'really busy' – resist the temptation to make it a contest. If you have the time, ask them to tell you about it … no, really, to tell you about it. Your listening and support might be just what they need.

KPIs – what are they good for?

What proportion of your working week is consumed by

creating reports, updates, responses to KPIs and other tasks of that kind? More importantly, what proportion of your working week is spent creating reports, updates and responses to KPIs that **actually add value**?

Yes, we need to keep track of progress – but seriously, how many weekly, fortnightly and monthly reports is too many? And, given the structure of many organisations, once these reports are consolidated and sanitised for senior consumption, how accurate are they anyway. Are they presenting the true state of play or presenting an upward impression that might be less than 100% accurate?

As I write this, I recall a program I worked on several years ago – around 1200 people with seven levels of reporting and leadership between me and the Program Director. We were all brought together every three months for an update and a pep talk. On one occasion, the Program Director stood up and told us how incredibly proud she was that on 'every single measure and KPI' that we report on, we were 'green lights' all the way. The interesting thing about this was that everyone I spoke to at my level told me that just about every one of their measures and KPIs were red.

Clearly somewhere between the coal face and the boss, the information was being consolidated and, apparently, adjusted to present a view that was more favourable than the reality. If the Program Director had been able to see what was really going on at each individual team level and was then able to take appropriate action, the program may not have failed and fallen over, wasting a vast amount of money.

Think about the organisation you work for, particularly if it is a larger company. No doubt there are requirements around training. And probably completing performance appraisals and development conversations. Hopefully, there are also measures that relate to health and safety performance. If you are working on a project, there are probably progress reports that need to be churned out regularly, often taking you away from the task at hand – that is, the successful delivery of the program of work. There are probably others that you can think of, too.

Now, ask yourself – **what are these performance measures actually good for?**

Are training programs being offered to genuinely improve the organisation and the individual colleagues' capability or to tick a box – maybe a regulatory box? Are performance appraisals being used to genuinely develop the capability and career opportunities for the individual involved or to meet a completion requirement for the leader involved? Is the performance against the company's health and safety measures primarily used to genuinely improve the working environment or to contribute to the annual bonus calculations? Are the project reports being used to ensure that everything is on track or as an opportunity to strip some funding out of that program and into another?

If you can say, hand on heart, that the measures are being used for the purpose they were intended, congratulations! That sounds like a great place to work – I encourage you to keep on reporting!

If not, it brings us back to the original question – **KPIs – what are they good for?**

*** With acknowledgement to Edwin Starr for the title, adapted from his song 'War – What Is It Good For' from the 1970 album, 'War And Peace'*

When milestones become millstones

The phrase 'a millstone around your neck' literally goes back to Biblical times and has evolved into an expression that relates to a heavy burden or inescapable responsibility.

While I acknowledge that milestones are an important part of delivering any project, I find that for some change practitioners, they become more important than the actual outcomes associated with them.

You might be thinking that it is important to meet milestones if we are going to deliver the program of work and I absolutely agree. It is when they become **more** important than the outcomes that I have a problem.

I have worked on projects where the only important measure is the ticking off of milestones. Often this occurs because we made a promise to a steering committee or someone who needs to make sure that the budget is under control or something similar.

Have you ever worked on a project where a decision was made to go-live with a cut-down version of the agreed outcome? What about a project where we add the word 'lite' or 'pilot' because we ran out of time and delivering against a milestone was seen to be more important?

Yes, there are times where pilot versions or light versions of the full change are important steps, maybe as a proof-of-concept. But when these decisions are made in the light of a project running behind schedule, just so that we can say we met a milestone, I'm not so sure that this is a good approach.

By all means, change your schedule, reduce or adjust scope or take other steps to meet timelines. Do it because it makes sense. Do it because the agreed destination has changed. Do it because business conditions have moved.

Just don't do it to meet a milestone. Don't let milestones become millstones.

How long is too long?

I recently read about someone who had just completed 50 years of service for their company. **50 years!** Wow! Well done, her.

But, upon reflection, I wondered whether I should be impressed or concerned for her and the company she works for.

Let's take the positive approach and consider how much she has contributed to the organisation that she has called home for the past 50 years. That's something like 11,250 days at work or close enough to 90,000 hours of her life spent working for and investing energy and effort into the same organisation. She would have witnessed so many changes over the years. Given that she started in the 1970s, it means she would have seen the introduction of fax machines (remember those?), a computer for each person, call centres, mobile phones, working from home, teleconferencing and so much more. Likewise, she would have seen the demise of shorthand, smoking in the office, fax machines (remember those?), typing pools and a range of other features of office life in the 70s, 80s and 90s.

But is working for the same organisation for a long, long, long time a good thing?

Yes, it shows commitment and it shows loyalty. But does it suggest ongoing growth, breadth of experience, opportunities to step outside of comfort zones? I think not. At what point does loyalty become laziness? At what point does feeling comfortable become stale?

So, addressing the initial question – how long is too long? Is working in the same role for three years too long? Is working for the same organisation for ten years too long? Don't forget that long service leave typically kicks in at ten years, so that must be considered long service!

I am by no means being critical or judgmental nor do I have the answer that is the right answer for everyone – indeed, I am just asking the question.

How long is too long?

Leave the door open

There is an old saying that says **opportunity knocks but once** – but does it even knock once?

I go back to a time in the late 1980s when I had decided to leave teaching to try something different. I had done all of the 'normal things' to find something new to do. I had responded to job ads, spoken to members of my network, etc. but, try as I might, I simply couldn't find a new opportunity anywhere.

By the time we got to Christmas, I had resigned myself to going back into the classroom the following year and giving up on my goal of finding something different to do. Being Christmas, I went along to a family party and found myself sitting next to a distant relative who, I found out after half an hour of small talk, was also a teacher. When comparing notes, I explained what I had hoped to do during the following school year. Her surprising response was that, during the day before, she had caught up with an old teaching colleague who had done exactly what I wanted to do – leave teaching for at least twelve months to try a different type of job. She was starting to despair that she wasn't going to find anyone to join her team for an upcoming project – ideally a teacher, who wanted to step out for a year.

Before I left the party, I had spoken to the person who ultimately became my first non-teaching boss. And here, I am, thirty-plus years later, still working outside of teaching.

Opportunity didn't knock … I just happened to stumble onto

exactly what I was looking for. The door must have been open at the time.

Are you waiting for an opportunity to find you? Are you sitting, waiting, hoping that at some stage, someone will open your door and offer you the opportunity of a lifetime? If you are, alas, I fear that you will still be sitting, waiting, hoping for many days and weeks to come. Yes, occasionally, the opportunity will come to you. Far, far more often you'll need to be proactively looking for that opportunity.

If I were you, I'd leave the door open and watch what passes by rather than hoping that it will stop and knock.

Customer centric or organisational centric?

Don't you love reading about organisations that say that they are customer-centric, customer-focussed, customer-obsessed or something similar?

We hear lots of noise from companies about listening to their customers and creating products and services that match their needs.

But here is a challenge – what are **YOU** doing to really embrace your customer needs and preferences? What is your organisation doing to listen to and act upon what the customer wants?

Yes, you can tell me about customer surveys or NPS scores. They are a satisfactory snapshot in time of how a small sample of customers are feeling. They'll give you a score and maybe a comment about how they are feeling, but rarely does the survey include an opportunity to suggest a change.

There has been what seems to be an exponential increase in the number of these surveys that are sent out via email or SMS after an interaction with an organisation. Whether that is a service organisation, a shop or some other business, the survey arrives two days later only asking you to give a score out of 10.

And if you don't respond, there is often an automated follow-up request to complete the survey.

Stop and consider that for a moment – a single score in response to a question like 'would you recommend our services to friends or family'. How is that providing feedback?

Clearly, the automated response says that these numbers are being collected and collated into some kind of score. If I have provided a score of 3, what follow up is going to be done to see why the low score has been provided? I suspect none.

I have worked in places where the customer input is used for nothing more than calculating bonuses. You know when that happens – the salesperson, consultant or other customer service person tells you there is a survey on its way and that it would be absolutely amazing if you could give them a 9 or 10. That's all about providing data for a quantitative program that measures organisational and individual performance based purely on a number.

If we are seriously customer-centric, then surely, we want to have proper feedback and suggestions, not tainted by the pleas of the customer-facing folk, asking for exceptional ratings.

Let's suppose you have some kind of input mechanism where customers have a voice – a proper voice – where they can make suggestions and provide feedback and ideas for improvement. **Is this not the greatest gift to any organisation?**

So, the ideas come through and a great idea is discovered.

Be honest with yourself. Which is going to have the most influence on whether the change is made – the cost of implementing the change or the positive outcome it might have on the customer experience (please don't call it CX.

Calling it CX is like calling your colleagues HR – see above).

From my experience, the cost of change wins that argument just about everywhere.

I'm not saying that this is a bad thing. Costs need to be managed. Shareholders and owners need a return on their investment.

But let's call it out – most organisations are shareholder/owner centric. In most organisations, customer centricity is a distant second.

What is your dislodgement strategy?

This is closely related to other sections of the book that talk about inertia.

Think about your marketing strategy – what is that you are doing or offering to make your product appealing to a prospective customer or client.

If the service or product you are promoting is something new, something that these potential customers have never had the need for until now, your marketing strategy should, I guess, be focused on how the potential customer will benefit from using your product or service and how their lives will be enhanced. They'll never want to use anything else!

But what about products and services that already exist – banking services, cars, clothing brands, wines … the list is endless.

This is where your **dislodgement** strategy comes into view.

We have spoken about personal and organisational inertia throughout the book – the tendency for people or organisations to continue doing what they have always done.

If you have never bought a widget before, I only need to create a compelling argument that you need my widget. If I can convince you that your life will be better when you use a widget, you are very likely to become my latest customer.

But if you are already using a widget – one sold by my competitor – I don't have to convince you that using a widget is a good thing to do. I have to convince you that **my** widget is better than the one you are using.

Going back to the question of inertia, we know that your prospective customer is very likely to do exactly what they have always done. Metaphorically sitting in their bean bag, feeling very comfortable, just doing what they have always done.

So, what are you going to do to **dislodge** them from their inertial state?

The marketing strategy that outlines why your product is better than your competitor's product only becomes relevant when you have got that potential customer out of their bean bag.

What **dislodges** them?

If you can't answer that, they will probably keep on doing what they have always done – no new customer for you.

The Rectangle of Successful Completion

I was a mathematics teacher in the 1980s (note – I was sometimes a maths teacher, I was NEVER a **math** teacher!) and so I often try to explain things in terms of a mathematics concept.

Think about a rectangle on a vertical and horizontal axis – the horizontal axis representing time and the vertical axis being effort required. The area of that rectangle – that is, the likelihood of a successful outcome – equals the time available multiplied by the effort required.

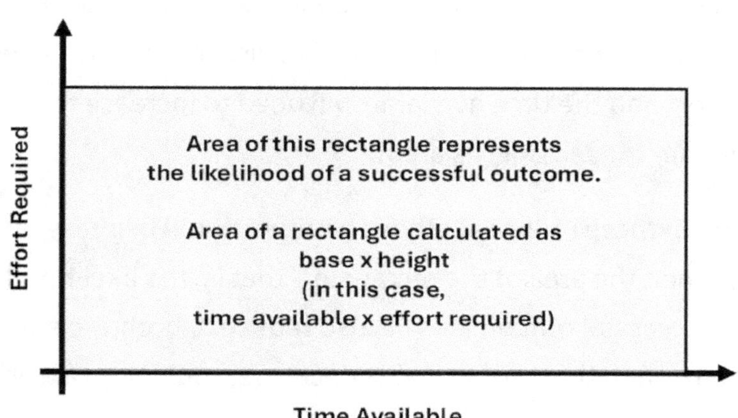

Given that the area of that rectangle tells us how likely we are to achieve success, consider this – if we reduce the time available, we need to increase the effort required to maintain that rectangular area. That is, if we reduce the number of days available by introducing delays or bringing the go-live date forward, we will, by definition, need to increase the amount of effort required.

Typically, this means increasing the number of people working on the project or, far more likely in my experience, expect the same number of people to do more.

The other consideration is this – if we reduce the effort (typically by reducing the number of people, having them move onto other projects, give the same people other tasks on top of what they are already doing, etc), to maintain the area of that rectangle, we'll need to allow more time.

Reduce the time available and you'll need to increase the effort by a proportional amount. Likewise, reduce the level of effort and the time available will need to increase to maintain the rectangle's area.

If one of these reduces without a proportional increase in the other, the area of the rectangle – that is, the likelihood of a successful outcome – will also reduce. If both the effort required and the time available decrease, you'll be in a world of pain.

Why keep hiring from the same industry?

I am fascinated by how organisations recruit, especially when it comes to recruiting people for a transformation program.

By definition, transformation is about changing things completely. We want things to function in a totally new way. I like to think of transformation as being the home ground of innovation.

And yet, far more often than not, you look at the job advertisements on what seems to be a growing number of job board web sites and there it is – candidates must have 5, 10 or more years of experience in the same sector.

How is a bank going to truly transform if they only recruit from the financial services sector? How is a government department going to truly transform if one of the key recruitment criteria is extensive experience in government roles? If transport companies only recruit people who have delivered programs of work in other transport companies, where are the innovative ideas coming from?

If you recruit exclusively from competitor organisations, there is a very good chance that any proposed innovation will, in fact, be more of the same.

I am not suggesting that we throw out the experience that SMEs can bring to the table but if we only rely on people who have done this work in a similar environment throughout their career, more of the same is the best we can hope for.

If you are a bank that wants to transform, recruit people from the retail sector – they'll know how to take your products and services to the people. If you are a government department looking to transform, bring in some people with corporate experience to provide you with a totally different outlook on running an organisation. If you are running a distribution business, look to people who have operational experience that doesn't only include transport.

Different perspectives are typically required to deliver

innovation – a mix of people with sector knowledge AND knowledge and experience from other sectors.

If you are seriously committed to recruiting from within your own sector, I would suggest that you are not really wanting transformation or innovation.

Chapter 7

And before I go – let's see what AI says

As I sit here writing this book, Artificial Intelligence is making headway in all sorts of arenas – corporate, education, music and the arts. I did promise at the start that everything in the book would be my words, unedited and presented as though I was sitting talking to you.

But, in the spirit of looking forward, I asked a couple of AI applications to explain how they encapsulated the concept of **Transformagination®**.

In each case, I asked the application the same question – 'What Is **Transformagination®**'. Here's how they summarised it.

What ChatGPT said

'**Transformagination**® seems to blend "transformation" and "imagination", suggesting a concept or business focused on creative change or innovative evolution. The term suggests a focus on bold, creative thinking – something that merges vision and action.'

What ChatGate AI said

'**Transformagination**® is a concept that promotes a new way of thinking, emphasising creativity and innovation beyond traditional methods of change. It encourages individuals and organisations to envision possibilities without the constraints often imposed by corporate inertia. Unlike incremental change, which is reactive and limited by existing rules, **Transformagination**® advocates for a proactive approach that fosters true creativity in redesigning business practices and strategies.

The term emerged from discussions among colleagues who recognised the need for a deeper shift beyond minor adjustments for their clients, leading to its establishment as a registered trademark. **Transformagination**® represents an opportunity to dream and reimagine possibilities without being bound by conventional thinking.'

What Perplexity said

'**Transformagination**® is a concept that combines transformation and imagination, promoting a mindset shift from conventional thinking to innovative possibilities. It encourages individuals and *organizations* (sic) to envision their goals and dreams without being hindered by existing constraints or traditional methods.'

Key Principles of Transformagination®

- Possibility-Driven Thinking: **Transformagination**® emphasises starting with aspirations and working backward to determine how to achieve them, rather than being limited by current circumstances or traditional approaches. This approach fosters creativity and the exploration of new ideas.

- Challenging Conventional Mindsets: The concept advocates for breaking free from corporate inertia and outdated practices. It encourages individuals to 'burn the box,' meaning to abandon conventional frameworks and explore unconventional solutions.

- Collaboration and Engagement:

Transformagination® promotes working collaboratively with clients and stakeholders, ensuring that everyone involved is engaged in the transformation process. This collaborative approach enhances creativity and innovation.

- Focus on Outcomes: Unlike traditional consulting, which may prioritise processes, **Transformagination**® emphasises achieving desired outcomes through innovative problem-solving.

Transformagination® can be applied in various contexts, including business strategy development, change management, and creative problem-solving. It encourages organisations to rethink their operations and strategies in light of new possibilities, ultimately leading to more effective and innovative solutions.

In summary, **Transformagination**® represents a progressive mindset that integrates imagination with transformation, enabling individuals and *organizations* (sic) to envision new possibilities and achieve their goals without the limitations imposed by traditional thinking.

And one last thing ...

In an earlier section of the book, I offered **The Window Conundrum** where a square window, measuring 1 metre across and 1 metre top to bottom was made twice the size, remained a square and was still 1 metre across and 1 metre from top to bottom.

This speaks to perception and the ability to think creatively. Here's a picture of the before and after:

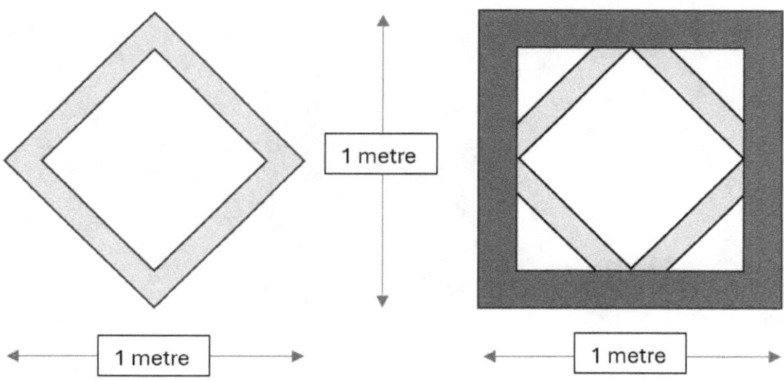

Our brains hear about a square window and visualise it being horizontal but, in fact it was rotated 45 degrees. By cutting the window as shown on the right, there is twice as much space cut out and yet, the horizontal and vertical measurements are STILL 1 metre and 1 metre.

Don't be constrained by what appears to be normal. Think,

literally in this case, outside the square!

About the Author

Neil Butler

Neil Butler is an Australian author, broadcaster and business founder whose career has been built around helping people navigate uncertainty with confidence and optimism.

Drawing on decades of experience across education, corporate leadership, small business, and media, he has developed a distinctive, practical approach to organisational and personal transformation. In his work, Neil blends clear-eyed realism about the pace of change with a playful curiosity about what might be possible if we dared to imagine something different.

Change Change and The Art of Transformagination® distils Neil's core philosophy – that meaningful change is less about highly structured methodologies and protocols and more about everyday mindset, language and behaviour.

Through stories, frameworks and questions that are intentionally simple but quietly provocative, he invites readers to reframe their relationship with change from something that 'happens to us' into something we can design, influence and even enjoy.

Away from the keyboard, Neil is known as an engaging speaker and host, trusted by audiences for his plain-language style, genuine warmth and willingness to challenge conventional thinking without losing his sense of humour.

When he is not writing or speaking about change, he can often be found behind a microphone, in conversation with people doing interesting work in their communities and organisations.

Change Change is his latest contribution to an ongoing career dedicated to helping people think differently, act deliberately and create better futures on purpose.